John Chisum

Frontier Cattle King

By

Bill O'Neal

EAKIN PRESS ◆ Fort Worth, Texas
www.EakinPress.com

Copyright © 2018
By Bill O'Neal
Published By Eakin Press
An Imprint of Wild Horse Media Group
P.O. Box 331779
Fort Worth, Texas 76163
1-817-344-7036
www.EakinPress.com
ALL RIGHTS RESERVED
1 2 3 4 5 6 7 8 9
ISBN-10: 1-68179-113-7
ISBN-13: 978-1-68179-113-5

Dedicated to

Bill Neal

*Texas Cowboy, Rancher, Attorney
and Distinguished Author*

Contents

Acknowledgments

I first researched and wrote about John Chisum for my book, *Historic Ranches of the Old West*, which was published in 1997. I visited the South Spring Ranch site near Roswell, thanks to the assistance of Morgan and Joyce Nelson, whose home was on property formerly owned by Pitser Chisum, younger brother of John. I was captivated by John Chisum, and I wrote about the cattle king in later books and articles.

I knew that the most meticulous research about Chisum had been accomplished by Harwood P. Hinton, who had accumulated information on the cattle king for half a century. As program chair for a meeting of the East Texas Historical Association in Paris, Chisum's home as a youngster and his burial site, I invited Dr. Hinton to provide a keynote address. I was highly impressed by the depth of his knowledge about Chisum. After his death in 2016, his papers were donated to the Southwest Collection at Texas Tech University. I contacted an old friend, Tai Kreidler, Librarian of the Southwest Collection and Executive Director of the West Texas Historical Association. Tai informed me that the Hinton papers had not yet been cataloged, but he encouraged me to contact Monte Monroe, Archivist of the Southwest Collection. Monte generously welcomed me to Lubbock and permitted me to examine the eighteen boxes containing the Hinton materials. I am deeply grateful to Monte and Tai.

During previous projects, I had researched at the Aikin Regional Archives at Paris Junior College, and I was ably assisted on each occasion by Daisy Harvill, Director of the Archives. I drove to Paris and visited Daisy, and she rapidly produced an array of expertly arranged files, inviting me to indicate which documents I wanted to be copied. Within a week I received a large packet from the Aikin Archives, and once more I've become indebted to Daisy Harvill. Nearby, at Texas A&M University in Commerce, I visited the archive section of the Gee Library, where I was skillfully assisted by Archivist Michael Barera. On short notice, Michael located key sources for me, and I'm grateful for his genial professionalism.

My research also was richly rewarded by the trip to the Haley Memorial Library and Museum in Midland, Texas. Years earlier I had enjoyed a most fruitful trip for another biographical project, so I sent a message to the director of the Haley Library, J.P. "Pat" McDaniel. On the day I arrived at the Haley Library, Archivist Cathy Smith was out of town, but director McDaniel took time from his busy schedule to collect and place in front of me a wealth of materials. I worked for four hours examining these materials and indicating copies and photos I needed. A few days later I received a call from Archivist Cathy Smith, discussing my visit and making sure she understood my order. Over the next few days we exchanged several calls, and a few days later I received a bulging packet with document copies and images. I made a final call to Cathy to thank her for her efforts on my behalf.

In Santa Fe at the Fray Angelica Chavez History Library, I met Senior Cataloguer Patricia Hewitt. Our appointment was prearranged, and she had books and document files already laid out for me. We had only two hours before Patricia had to attend a meeting, so she manned the copier while I rapidly assessed and indicated which items I needed. Thanks to her energetic assistance, I was able to finish my work within the allotted time.

When I commenced this project I sought out a visit with Bill Neal at his Abilene home. Bill was raised on a cattle ranch near Quanah, and as a young man, he cowboyed out of state. Today he owns a ranch near his old homeplace. He later became an attorney for forty years. Bill always was interested in the flamboyant history of frontier lawyers, and after he retired from his practice, he penned a series of excellent non-fiction books. Because of his background as a cowboy and rancher, I wanted to explore his impression of John Chisum. I asked a number of questions, and Bill provided me with thought-provoking insights. I am indebted to Bill O. Neal, who calls me "Apostrophe," while I address him as "Period." Many thanks, Period.

I sat beside Judge Tom Crum at a banquet of the East Texas Historical Association in Galveston. When I mentioned that I was working on a biography of John Chisum, he informed me that his grandmother had married into the Waide family. James Waide eventually purchased Chisum's ranch house near Bolivar. During Tom Crum's youth, his grandmother's house was near Chisum's former home, which belonged to another Waide relative. Tom described the Chisum home in detail to me and responded informatively to a bevy of questions I had about the house.

Two of my granddaughters, Chloe and Jessie Martinez, offered welcome assistance. Jessie, who studies art, created a drawing at my request of a longhorn with Jinglebob earmarks, while Chloe took a photo for me of the grave of John B. Denton. I appreciate their help. I received a book and other materials from James B. Hays of Early, Texas. I'm indebted for his generosity to a stranger.

At Panola College, Librarian Sherri Baker obtained several obscure books on interlibrary loan. I have benefited from her detective work on numerous projects, and Sherri always locates books for me with enthusiasm and skill. Another member of the library staff is Shay Joines, a young woman who cheerfully agreed to produce a manuscript for me and who adeptly solved every technological problem we encountered. Shay's efforts on this book were invaluable.

Chapter One

Introduction to a Cattle King

*"He had the knack of taking advantage of
any opportunity coming his way."*

— Lily Klasner

His name was John Simpson Chisum. But when he was a boy he was called "Cow John," because of his affinity for the cattle on his grandfather's Tennessee plantation. After becoming an open range rancher, Chisum was plagued by rustlers, and he developed a distinctive and unmistakably recognizable earmark known as "Jinglebob." Chisum soon was being called "Jinglebob John" and "Jinglebob Chisum." As his herds grew to vast numbers, he became known as the "Jinglebob King." A genial and prominent man, Chisum often was affectionately called "Uncle John," as well as "Old Chisum" — although probably not to his face. With his great New Mexico ranch stretching about 200 miles along the Pecos River, and with his cattle holdings numbering 60,000 to 80,000 head, Chisum became widely known as the "Cattle King of the Pecos," the "Stock King of New Mexico," the "Cattle King of the West," and most regal of all, the "Cattle King of America."[1]

John Chisum was destined to become cow country royalty. He began ranching at the dawn of the range cattle industry in Texas. Within a few years his cattle were numbered in the tens of thousands, and within a few more years Chisum owned more cattle than any other individual in America. His Jinglebob herds were the only cattle in the West known by an earmark rather than by a famous brand. Chisum was a true pioneer, seeking open range grass farther and farther and still farther west. His last ranch was the biggest, and he built a headquarters complex worthy of a frontier cattle king. Chisum relished the role of cattle baron, serving as a gracious and generous host to one and all.

During three decades on a succession of frontier ranches, Chisum endured Indian raids, stock thievery, drought, financial reverses, and the murderous conflict known as the Lincoln County War. He met every challenge head-on, hanging rustlers, taking losses of money and even of entire herds in stride, then forging ahead without complaint. Once, according to legend, Chisum faced down a lethal threat from Billy the Kid. Chisum had courage, a taste for adventure, a shrewd head for business, and he confidently operated his risky frontier profession on an enormous scale. After thirty spectacular years as a western rancher, Chisum died at sixty, just as his beloved open range was being enclosed by barbed wire. But John Chisum has never been forgotten in the world of ranching.

This future cattle king was born August 16, 1824, in Hardeman County in western Tennessee. His parents were Claiborne and Lucinda Chisum, and he was greeted by a two-year-old sister, Nancy. Nancy and John were joined by three brothers, all born in Hardeman County. James was born in 1827, Jeff in 1829, and Pitser in 1834. Claiborne Chisum and his father, James, a former state senator, ventured into western Tennessee as surveyors. Hardeman County was surveyed and organized in 1823, with the seat of government in Bolivar. A rural wilderness, Hardeman County registered a population of just 11,655 in the Census of 1830.[2]

It was customary for frontier surveyors to receive all or part of their compensation in land, and Claiborne and his father both established farms in Hardeman County. James Chisum's operation grew large enough to be termed a plantation with as many as seventeen slaves and a saw mill. As he aged (he was born in 1774 in Virginia) his son Claiborne managed the property, along with his own 800-acre farm. As Claiborne's sons grew, they were expected to help with the countless chores at their home place and their grandfather's plantation.[3]

From a young age, John Chisum worked as well as played outdoors. He developed a deep love and need for outdoor life, as well as a feel for the rhythms of agriculture and an understanding of livestock that produced the nickname "Cow John."

Schooling for frontier children was haphazard. There were one-room log school houses all over Tennessee, but teachers had to be found, often an unmarried young "schoolmarm," or a "perfessor" who taught school only until he could find something better. In 1812 nineteen-year-old Sam Houston, who as a boy had attended classes for less than a year, opened a school in a one-room log structure near Marysville in eastern Tennessee. Young Houston was a habitual reader, however, and he was an energetic teacher. But as soon as he paid off personal debts with tuition fees, he left teaching after one term.[4] Indeed, frontier school terms were brief, usually only three or four months, and often in the winter, when there was not as much to do on the farm.

There is no record or account of Chisum children attending a Hardeman County school, but such records from that era are scant. When no school was available to pioneer children, literate mothers usually taught the "3 R's—Readin', 'Ritin', and 'Rithmetic" - in the home. If there was no other book in a farm cabin, there was usually a copy of the King James Bible (the Chisums were Presbyterians), which could be used as a speller and grammar, as well as a source of ancient history and of morals, Good vs. Evil. Furthermore, since colonial times, pewter children's cups had been available with the alphabet engraved on the side—a pioneer learning aid.

Whether through a few short school terms or by lessons in

the home, bright children would learn the Three R's—and John Chisum was a highly intelligent child. Young John mastered the alphabet, began to recognize short letter words ("he", "we", "me", "the"), and learned to read. His spelling remained inexact, perhaps an embodiment of the theory of fellow Tennessean Andrew Jackson: " It's a damn poor mind that can think of only one way to spell a word."[5]

Chisum developed a neat, readable handwriting style, as shown by surviving samples. And when he learned the basics of arithmetic, a mathematical gift was unlocked that would be of constant use to him as a rancher. Legendary cattleman Charles Goodnight later said with admiration that Chisum "was the best counter I ever knew. He could count three grades of cattle at once, and count them accurately even if they were going in a trot."[6]

Chisum also had musical talent. He learned to play the fiddle, a skill that he happily used at country dances and, later, at ranch celebrations. He enjoyed parties and dances and all manner of social occasions. Young Chisum laughed easily and often, a trait that he maintained throughout his life, and he enjoyed practical jokes.[7]

There was a strong pioneering tradition among Tennesseans, and throughout John Chisum's boyhood, a parade of frontiersmen migrated from Tennessee to Texas, which had been opened to Anglo settlers in 1821. By 1835 Texans were in rebellion against Mexico and its dictatorial *presidente*, Antonio Lopez de Santa Anna. In the spring of 1836, General Santa Anna overwhelmed and massacred the rebel garrison at the Alamo in San Antonio. More than thirty Tennesseans perished at the Alamo, including David Crockett, a famed bear hunter and former congressman who, when defeated by voters, defiantly announced, "You all can go to hell, I'm going to Texas."

Santa Anna led his army deep into Anglo Texas, and settlers abandoned their homes and fled in desperation. But General

Sam Houston, an even more famous Tennessean than David Crockett, executed a strategic retreat with his ragtag army before turning and leading a spectacular triumph at the Battle of San Jacinto. Houston's mentor was the most famous Tennessean of all, President Andrew Jackson. As a young army officer under General Jackson, Houston was a wounded hero of the Battle of Horseshoe Bend. Later he served Tennessee as congressman and governor, and in the wake of San Jacinto, Houston was overwhelmingly elected the first president of the Republic of Texas.

With Texas no longer a part of Mexico, with Tennesseans martyred heroes of the Texas Revolution, with Tennessean Sam Houston now in charge of the new Texas Republic, the parade of Tennessee migrants surged in 1836. Among the parade of Texas-bound pioneers from Tennessee was Claiborne Chisum and his family. Friends and former neighbors already had moved to Texas, settling in the Red River District in the northeast area of the Lone Star Republic, which had promised free land to new migrants.

Early in the fall of 1837 Claiborne supervised the packing of household goods and farm implements into covered wagons. Claiborne's friend and attorney, Pitser Miller (his namesake, Pitser Miller Chisum, was John's youngest brother) was charged with selling the Chisum property. Departing on September 25, the first leg of the trek was less than sixty miles west to Memphis, where the Chisum wagons were ferried across the mile-wide Mississippi River. The trail angled southwest through Little Rock and across Arkansas, 270 miles or more, with a three-day crossing of the Red River at Ragsdale's Ferry.[8]

It was the first great adventure a young John's life. The thirteen-year-old crossed the great Mississippi, camped out in new territory every night, helped tend the family livestock, took his turn at the reins of the wagons. John Chisum had taken part in a pioneer experience of America's westward movement, and later in life, he would not hesitate to seek new frontiers.

At first, the Chisum family stayed close to the Red River Valley while Claiborne investigated property possibilities. The Red River District was a vast province that eventually would be divided into thirty-nine counties. In December 1837 the Texas Republic created sprawling Red River County, which comprised all or part of nine future counties, including Lamar County. It was in this county of the future that Claiborne Chisum decided to settle. Early in 1838 he bought 2,085 acres for $10,000 from an early migrant and filed for a nearby grant of 1,280 acres from the Texas Republic.[9]

Sadly, Lucinda Chisum died a few months earlier, on October 31, 1837. She was only thirty-three, and she passed away of some unidentified malady in Clarksville, seat of Red River County. Claiborne, having already begun the process of securing a site for the new family home, placed Lucinda's remains in a grave on a hill a few hundred yards south of his future residence.[10] John Chisum was only thirteen when he lost his mother, and he became a responsible and protective big brother to James, Jeff, and Pitser.

Claiborne kept his sons busy. Pitser was only three, but the older boys helped build the new house, as well as outbuildings. The residence was a typical double log cabin, with a dog run between the two main rooms and a sleeping loft upstairs. With the death of her mother, fifteen-year-old Nancy became the woman of the house, perhaps aided by one of the female servants. But two years later in 1839, Nancy married B.J. Bourland at the new Chisum residence. It was the first wedding held at what would become the townsite of Paris.[11]

With a house full of children, Claiborne Chisum needed a wife. In 1840 he married Cynthia Latimer, a widow from Clarksville. Claiborne was eighteen years her senior, and he instructed his children to call her "Aunt Cynthia." Cynthia was twenty-five, and she brought two little boys to the marriage.

Claiborne and Cynthia had four children of their own: Robert, Laura, Mary, and John, of course, was their half-brother, and apparently his step-mother Cynthia created a warm environment in her new home. Years later, in New Mexico, John made it clear to a friend "that he always held her in the greatest affection even though he was far away from her."[12]

George W. Wright had settled years earlier in the Red River District, and he served the Republic of Texas as a congressman. Anticipating congressional authorization of the "Central National Road," from Dallas to the Red River at Jonesborough, as well as a statute to locate the seat of county government within five miles of the geographical center of each county, Wright moved from Pecan Point on the Red River to the future Lamar County.

George W. Wright donated the townsite for Paris, staying at the Chisum home while he explored the area. *Photo by the author*

Wright stayed at the home of Claiborne Chisum when he first explored the area in 1839. Congress established the new county in December 1840, and an election organized Lamar County on February 1, 1841. The seat of government at first was uncertain, but Wright had purchased 1,000 acres from which he donated fifty acres for what became the site of the town - and county seat - of Lamar County. Claiborne Chisum's home was on the southwestern edge of the new townsite of Paris. When Paris was platted, Washington Street ran between the Chisum house and family cemetery.[13]

As the community of Paris began to grow around the town square, the nearest water supply was from Mud Creek, which ran near the Chisum home. Teenaged John "earned a very tidy sum" by hauling water to the town. After he told about "his first business venture" to a young lady who knew him as a New Mexico cattle king, she reflected: "He had the knack of taking advantage of any opportunity coming his way."[14]

There were Indian raids in the vicinity during 1837 and 1838, and newly arrived Claiborne Simpson led a six-man squad of riders as part of a volunteer pursuit partly in June 1838. For four months late in 1838 and early in 1839 Claiborne was on the company roll of an area militia unit. And in the spring of 1841 Claiborne rode with a punitive expedition in response to continued raids, while sixteen-year-old John, the oldest son, was left in charge of protecting the family.[15] Several villages of Tonkawa, Caddo, and Cherokee Indians were clustered along a stream today called Village Creek in the modern city of Arlington. Republic of Texas President M.B. Lamar advocated an aggressive policy against Indians, and Colonel E.H. Tarrant of the Texas Militia was directed to lead a volunteer force against these villages. Claiborne Chisum was one of seventy men who mustered for "Tarrant's Expedition." Tarrant, a veteran of the Battle of New Orleans and of the Texas Revolution, led his riders southwest from Grayson County toward the approximate location of the village.[16]

Early on the morning of May 24, the Texan force jumped what turned out to be the southernmost village. The surprise attack routed the Indians, who fled up a trail leading north, downstream toward the Trinity River. Leaving several men to secure the captured village, Colonel Tarrant led a pursuit northward. After two miles another village was seized, and a third village was sighted below. But the warriors below had readied their weapons, and there was an exchange of fire. Colonel Tarrant's aide, Capt. John B. Denton, was aiming his rifle from horseback when a bullet struck him in the chest. Captain Denton, thirty-four and the father of six, died instantly, while two other men were wounded. Although a dozen braves were killed, a hasty count revealed 225 lodges, and the outnumbered Texans retired from the field.

Tarrant's men looted the deserted villages of thirty-seven horses, six cows, guns, gunpowder, lead, saddles, buffalo robes, and tools. On the second day after heading north toward Bonham, the company halted at a creek embankment to dig a grave with knives and tomahawks. A slate slab was placed atop John Denton's corpse, which had been wrapped in a blanket. Dirt was smoothed across the grave, and leaves were scattered so that Indians could not find the remains. A few months later Colonel Tarrant returned with a force of 400 men, but the villages had been abandoned. Within a few years adjoining counties were named after Colonel Tarrant and Captain Denton.

After returning home, Claiborne Chisum regaled his family about his adventure with Tarrant's Expedition, including details of Denton's burial. In the 1850s, when John began looking for an area to graze a herd of cattle, Claiborne described the promising country he had seen during the punitive expedition. And when John established his ranch in Denton County, with cattle ranging into Tarrant County, he would decide to seek the grave of Captain Denton.

As a pioneer settler who had ridden in defense of the new county, Claiborne Chisum actively sought opportunity as Paris developed during the 1840s. He acquired more land, bought a few additional slaves, helped start a school, and made livestock trades. In 1846 Lamar County voted to erect a two-story brick courthouse on the Paris town square, and Claiborne and his brother-in-law, Epps Gibbons (they had married sisters) acted as contractors. Among the workmen that they hired were sons John and James Chisum and Ed and John Gibbons. Epps Gibbons fired the bricks at a kiln near his house in the northwest part of town, and one of the tasks of John and other laborers was to haul bricks to the building site. Completed by the summer of 1847, a Fourth of July celebration was held in the new courthouse, with music provided by the town's first piano and,

quite likely, by the fiddle of John Chisum.[17]

Chisum continued to help his father on his farms. He worked on other construction projects—buildings and bridges—as the town grew. He clerked in stores, including the grocery of M.M. Grant. Wages were low, and so were profit margins. But even though he did not see his future in running a store, Chisum ap-

This structure is regarded by many as the Lamar County Courthouse which John Chisum helped to build in 1846. *Courtesy Lamar County Historical Museum.*

plied what he learned as a clerk to a series of ranch supply stores throughout his career as a frontier cattleman.[18]

During these years as a jack of all trades, Chisum was interested in a number of girls, "but they were all friends." A girl named Sue Holman caught his fancy—"She was what I call a harum-scarum type—not rough but full of mischief and ready for a joke at any and all times."[19]

In the fall of 1851, when he was nearly twenty-seven, Chisum wrote to a friend in Hardeman, Tennessee. After describing crops and weather, he mentioned that "I am selling groceries in Paris for M.M. Grant" and that "Brother James also is selling groceries" for another merchant. Chisum further related that "the youngsters are getting in the spirit of marrying." He described the recent wedding of his cousin, Frances Johnson, to Thomas Towery, and that two days of dancing followed the ceremony. Chisum then pointedly added, "as for my part I am in a big way of courting [Sue Holman?] and I can't tell how soon I may marry but I think soon."[20]

Following a lengthy courtship Chisum finally asked Sue Holman to marry. But a newcomer to Paris attracted her attention. "So I plunged deeper and deeper into work and tried to forget her." Sue soon married "that city dude and moved away to where he came from."[21]

The pattern for Chisum's romantic life was set. He enjoyed the company of young ladies, displaying a flirtatious nature throughout his life. But ultimately, he kept girls at arms' length. They remained just "friends" to him or, in later life, he befriended girls who were clearly too young for him. Sue Holman was "full of mischief and ready for a joke at any and all times"—and so was Chisum. But he delayed serious talk of marriage until she found someone else. He shrugged it off by saying that "nobody will have me." Regarding later sweethearts he would say with a laugh, "The girl didn't court me enough."[22]

He never married because he did not want to marry. John Chisum was deeply ambitious. "John loved money," concluded a woman who knew him later in life.[23] He had a fierce drive to achieve prosperity and prominence. As a young man he seemed aimless: farmhand, water hauler, construction laborer, store clerk. Nothing he tried was promising, especially not if he were saddled with a wife and children. He continued to seek the main chance, while avoiding marriage. His brothers and other relatives satisfied his love of family, and he welcomed brothers, nieces, nephews, and cousins to his circle.

At the age of twenty-six he decided to try politics. In 1850 John Chisum ran for the office of county clerk, but the incumbent, John R. Craddock, won by a small margin. After two more years of clerking and farm work, Chisum ran again in 1852, and this time he won.[24] The county clerk's office was on the first floor of the brick court house that Chisum had helped to construct a few years earlier. In England during the Middle Ages property transfers had to be recorded by clergymen, who were

The Sam Bell Maxey home in Paris is a State Historic Site. Maxey was a veteran of the Mexican War, a Confederate general, and a two-term U.S. senator. During the Civil War Jeff Chisum served as a corporal in a Home Guard company sponsored by General Maxey. *Photo by the author.*

virtually the only persons who could read and write. They were called "clericus," or "clerks." These clerks not only produced property documents, but because they could read and write they became "clerks to the courts," maintaining records of various court proceedings. Such duties evolved in the American colonies, and in Texas the county clerk acted as a recorder and custodian of important public records, including deeds, birth and death certificates, bonds, and livestock. The county clerk served as recorder and custodian of the county commissioners court, issued marriage licenses, and served as chief election officer.

All documents, including lengthy deeds, had to be recorded by hand. Jacob Long was the assistant to the Lamar County Clerk, and Chisum relied upon him heavily. But County Clerk Chisum found his duties onerous, and he despised spending the workday confined in an office. He later explained "that his health was beginning to suffer from the confining work," and he became less and less of a presence in the office. In effect Jacob Long finished the term, and he was elected county clerk in his own right in 1854.[25]

But while Chisum was in office, he learned a great deal about property transactions and real estate dealings. In fact, when property parcels were auctioned off for unpaid taxes, Chisum was an interested presence at the courthouse steps. He often picked up property bargains at these auctions.[26]

During this period John Chisum began buying steers and selling them to butchers in Paris and other new communities in the area. This business was profitable, and "Cow John"—older and more experienced now, but with the same affinity for cattle—began to see future possibilities in work that finally suited and challenged him.

Chapter Two

Cow John Becomes a Texas Cattleman

I got back from Vicksburg a few days since. I find the Prairies all burnt off and we have had no rain hear [sic] since last spring."
— John Chisum

John Chisum turned thirty in 1854. His two-year term as county clerk expired that year, but he had become disinterested in his duties and had no intention of running for re-election. Although he had worked at a variety of jobs since he was a teenager, he was still searching for something that offered the level of success that he craved. But by 1854 he had become aware of an economic activity that was developing in Texas that might offer limitless possibilities to men who were bold enough, courageous enough, imaginative enough to seize the chance.

Chisum had handled livestock on a small scale on his grandfather's plantation and his father's farm. He had acquired cattle to sell to butchers. It was reported that about 1850 Chisum "was one of the drivers employed by Henry and Abe Rhine, merchants in Paris, to drive to California a herd of cattle which was assembled on Grand Prairie in western Lamar County. . . ." This story seems dubious because in 1850 there was not yet a trail to California from Texas. A few years later herds were driven to California mining country along new stagecoach and military roads that did not exist in 1850, and Texas cattle brought as much as $100 apiece. But a cattle drive to California in 1850, across untracked mountains and deserts, would have been a famous and epic event. John Chisum never spoke of joining an early California cattle drive. The alleged California drive of 1850 must have been confused with a drive that the Rhine brothers launched toward California in 1855. Other cattle drives from Lamar County to California were put together in 1857 and 1858. But by 1855, as well as 1857 or 1858, John Chisum had left Lamar County to build his own cattle ranch to the west.[1]

There were great numbers of wild longhorns in South Texas. The area above the Rio Grande was harsh country that was largely uninhabited, but since the 1700s the Spanish had brought herds, large and small, up *El Camino Real*. This "Royal Road" led from Mexico City across the Rio Grande to San Antonio, then eastward to Spanish Florida. As the herds moved north, some of the cattle strayed into the brush country, where the lean, agile beasts became hardy survivors, finding water and foraging for food. They also were aggressive when fighting off predators, with their horns evolving into long, dangerous weapons. As they multiplied, some longhorns began to seek new feeding grounds to the north. During the 1850s longhorns multiplied exponentially, with an estimated total of 3.7 million head by the Census of 1860. Although Texas was the fastest-growing state in the Union during the 1850s, the 1860 population of 604,215 was only one-sixth the number of cattle grazing in the Lone Star State.

In 1846 Edward Piper trailed 1,000 cattle from Texas to Ohio, and sporadically there were other drives to Illinois, Missouri, Iowa, and Indiana. A few herds were driven through the swamplands of East Texas and lower Louisiana to New Orleans. Richard King and Miflin Kenedy began ranching operations in South Texas in 1853, and the King Ranch in particular expanded relentlessly. In 1855 Oliver Loving started a ranch in Palo Pinto County, and two years later Charles Goodnight began running cattle in the same county.

John Chisum was not the only man who noted these developments. Among the capitalists who recognized profit possibilities with cheap Texas cattle was Stephen K. Fowler. A native of New York, Fowler had accepted a position in New Orleans, where cattle had arrived from Texas. In 1854 Fowler traveled to Paris in search of a cattleman whom he could trust to purchase and tend a herd of cattle. He met Chisum, who told him where he would seek cattle and where he would range their herd. Chisum agreed to a ten-year partnership for a share of the profits, which could be paid in calves.[2]

Chisum rode to Colorado County in southeast Texas. The county seat is Columbus, and in the humid, warm climate cattle thrived. As Chisum learned more about the fledgling cattle business in Texas, he heard about a source of cattle in Colorado County. With Fowler's capital, he bought stock cattle at six dollars per head, with calves thrown in. Chisum and a crew of hired drovers trailed the herd of 1,200 animals north.[3]

Intrigued by his father's description of the country Claiborne had ridden over during the Indian troubles of 1841, Chisum headed for the ranges of Denton and Tarrant counties. He bought 220 acres of land where he would build a headquarters complex; then he turned the cattle loose to graze and to fend for themselves. Unlike ranchers such as King and Kenedy, who carefully acquired title to their ranch lands, Chisum decided to base his cattle operation on open range principles. There were vast rangelands in Texas and much of the rest of the West. The federal government controlled vacant lands in all states except Texas, which retained control of its public lands because of the unique terms of a republic joining the United States.

John Chisum reasoned that the most profitable approach to frontier ranching was grazing on open range. There would be no financial expenditure for land, except for a small plot for ranch headquarters. Cattle were cheap, grazing was free, and drovers were paid only about thirty dollars a month. Reproduction on the range would provide herd increase at no expense. If attractive markets were found the profits would be immense.

Of course, there were risks, and during his career, Chisum would experience all of them. But after years of working for low wages or slender profit margins, Chisum had found an occupation compatible with his tastes and temperament. Confident of his prospects, he was ready to accept risks. He found himself to be a risk-taking entrepreneur during a wide-open entrepreneurial age in America. The basic economic policy of the government was *laissez-faire*—to leave alone—and the free enterprise system was given full rein. Businessmen were unregulated, and taxes were low. As a cattleman/entrepreneur at just the right place and time, John Chisum would thrive.

The land he acquired for his headquarters featured a hill overlooking, to the east, a stream called Clear Creek. The surrounding countryside was open, and an approaching war party could be seen from a considerable distance. But warlike Indians had been cleared out years earlier. Fort Worth, established to the southwest in 1849, was abandoned by the army in 1853. Troops no longer were needed, and civilians moved into the vacant buildings, converting the parade ground to the town

John Chisum built his "Great White House" atop a hill with a commanding view of all approaches. The current residence was built in recent years on the identical site. *Photo by the author.*

square.

In 1854 Chisum erected a comfortable frame house atop the hill and painted it white. The "Great White House" on its commanding location attracted attention, and the sociable Chisum responded to the role of host. For the rest of his life his ranch home—in Denton County or at two locations in New Mexico Territory—would regularly provide meals to travelers and other guests. The final ranch home he built, in New Mexico, featured an outsized dining table and a nearby building for dances.

At the Great White House Chisum maintained a housekeeper. In 1858 he acquired a slave named Jensie from a first cousin and her husband, Frances and Tom Towery. Jensie brought three small children to the ranch, where she assumed the role of housekeeper. Jensie's oldest child was Phillip, born about 1851 or 1852. Her daughters, Harriett and Almeady, were born in 1855 and 1857. Jensie assumed "Chisum" for her last name, and it long was speculated that John Chisum was the father of Almeady and perhaps Harriett. Clifford Caldwell's biography, *John Simpson Chisum, The Cattle King of the Pecos*, features meticulous genealogical research which caused the author to conclude that Chisum almost certainly was not the father of any of Jensie's children. And when Chisum moved his ranch farther west during the 1860s, he placed Jensie and her children in living quarters in Bonham.[4]

The winter of 1854-55 was bitter, but Chisum held a Christmas dance for his crew and neighbors. His herd survived, and he began to add to it with small purchases and trades. Stephen Fowler provided more capital, and with it, Chisum found an incredible deal: 1,000 head of cattle for $2,000, and the herd was delivered to his ranch. The Census of 1860 recorded Chisum-Fowler cattle valued at $50,000, along with six slaves. He liked to point out that his cattle grazed on range as far southwest as Fort Worth. And cattle buyers began coming to purchase substantial herds of Chisum-Fowler cattle.[5]

Although Denton County was formed in 1846, there were few inhabitants and a permanent county sent was not determined for a decade. At last, in 1856, a settler donated 100 acres for a townsite in the center of the county, and in 1857 the village of Denton began to take shape. The new county seat developed about fifteen miles south of Chisum's ranch, and occasionally he rode into town. When the IOOF organized a lodge in 1859, John Chisum became a charter member of the Independent Order of Odd Fellows, Denton Lodge No. 82.[6]

John's father, Claiborne Chisum, died on October 24, 1857, at the age of sixty. Claiborne did not leave a will, and there were hard feelings between some of the older children and their stepmother, "Aunt Cynthia," over the inheritance. A disgruntled James Chisum even took a shot at his stepmother, nicking her shoulder. Although there was no prosecution, James moved with his wife and children away from Paris. There was an estate sale, at which John bought a wagon and 500 head of sheep. He understood as many other cattlemen would, that sheep provided two payoffs each year, the lamb crop and a wool clip. Chisum grazed his flock—which numbered 11,000 in 1860—in the northern part of "his" range. The family dispute over Claiborne's property went to court, and the final settlement was made in 1861. Cynthia Chisum was awarded the family home and other property valued at $15,216.99, while each of the children received property valued at $4,347.68.[7]

John Chisum did not often return to Paris, but he engaged a cousin, John Gibbons, to look after his property and business interests in the area.[8] For years Chisum rode across the range where his cattle grazed, checking on his animals and grass and water conditions. In 1856 some of his cowboys found a grave beside Oliver Creek in Denton County, and Chisum suspected that the body was that of John B. Denton. He had learned from his father and other veterans of the 1841 campaign that Denton had some gold teeth, and that an arm had been broken. A tin cup

JOHN B. DENTON

BORN IN TENNESSEE
JULY 26, 1806
CAME TO TEXAS IN JANUARY, 1836
AS A METHODIST CIRCUIT RIDER
KILLED IN THE VILLAGE CREEK INDIAN FIGHT
MAY 24, 1841
IN WHAT IS NOW TARRANT COUNTY
NAMED FOR
GEN. EDWARD H. TARRANT,
WHO COMMANDED THE VOLUNTEERS.
DENTON CITY AND COUNTY
WERE NAMED FOR THE
PIONEER LAWYER, PREACHER, SOLDIER
OF THAT NAME

Erected by the State of Texas
1936

Captain John B. Denton was slain in 1841 and buried by his comrades. In 1856 John Chisum found the remains and reinterred Denton behind the Great White House. In 1902 the remains again were moved, to the courthouse square of Denton County. *Photo by Chloe Martinez.*

and a few other small items were placed in the grave. When Chisum and other riders arrived at the grave, there were gold teeth and a tin cup and remnants of a blanket, and the skeleton included an arm bone that had been broken.[9]

The remains were placed in a box and taken to the Chisum ranch house. The box was interred behind the house. When Chisum moved away from Denton County, the ranch was acquired by J.M. Waide. Chisum left behind with a friend, J.W. Gober, a written account of the exhumation and reburial of John Denton. In 1900 the Old Settler's Association of Denton County placed a newspaper ad searching for the remains of Denton. Gober produced the letter from John Chisum, and the body again was exhumed. On November 21, 1901, amid solemn ceremonies, the remains of John B. Denton were interred in the southeast corner of the courthouse lawn. The magnificent 1896 Denton County courthouse still stands, and John B. Denton continues to rest in its shadow.[10]

Chisum had been ranching in Denton County for five years when a town began to develop less than three miles south of his hilltop home. As enough settlers moved near each other to justify a community, Dr. Hiram Daily, who doubled as a Methodist minister on Sundays, purchased the site. Daily laid out a town-site, opened a general store, and named the village New Prospect. Within a couple of years, in 1861, a new settler, farmer Ben Brown, proposed renaming the little community. Brown had moved from Bolivar, Tennessee, the seat of Hardeman County, John Chisum's boyhood home. Brown bought free drinks for the men of the town, and they cheerfully voted to rename the village Bolivar.[11]

By this time there were a few small ranches in the neighborhood, as well as new farms. Indeed, the area proved to be excellent farm country. John Chisum was busy during the first couple of years of the Civil War rounding up and driving cattle herds to Confederate troops. But with farmers and ranchers and townspeople a nearby presence, Chisum began to realize that his open range operation would become limited.

When Chisum brought his first herd to Denton County in 1854, the cattle carried the brand Half Circle P. Other brands were used by Chisum, including some which already had been applied by the previous owner of a herd. At some point Chisum began using a Long Rail brand, a straight mark burned on the left flank from shoulder to hip. The Long Rail became one of the most famous brands in the West.

Even more famous was the earmark that Chisum devised while ranching in Denton County. Inserting a knife just above the root of the ear, he cut upward, splitting the upper ear into two segments. One segment flopped downward, suggesting

Illustration of a jinglebobbed steer. *Courtesy of Jessica Martinez.*

two separate ears. Cowboys often liked to attach a set of trinkets to their spurs that jingled with every step. These trinkets were called "Jinglebobs." For his distinctive - and less than humane—earmarks,

Chisum used the term "Jinglebob," and his cattle became known throughout cow country as "Jinglebobs." With both ears altered, Jinglebobs could be spotted at any roundup herd or crowded corral. These were the only cattle known primarily by their earmark.

When the War Between the States erupted in 1861, John Chisum had one of the largest cattle herds in Texas. State officials designated him a supplier of beef for Confederate troops, and in October 1862 he was appointed Regimental Quartermaster and Commissary, 21st Brigade of State Troops.[12] This role suited Chisum perfectly. He had no interest in fighting a war, but he had a great deal of beef to sell to soldiers.

Meanwhile, John's brothers also served in various Texas units. James was a member of Company K of the Texas Dismounted Cavalry, Second Texas Partisan Rangers. Dismounted Cavalry companies had no horses and functioned as infantry, but they preferred to be called "Cavalry." Pitser was a Quartermaster Sergeant of the Nineteenth Regiment of Texas Infantry, and he saw action during the Red River Campaign of 1864.[13]

Although Jeff was an epileptic with a frail physique, he served as a corporal in Maxey's Company of the Lamar Rifles. General Samuel Bell Maxey was a prominent citizen of Paris. An 1846 graduate of West Point, Maxey distinguished himself during the Mexican War, before leaving the army to become an attorney. Throughout the Civil War Maxey held several important

A jinglebob "trinket" attached to a spur. *Photo by the author.*

commands, and he also sponsored a Home Guard company. The health problems of Corporal Jeff Chisum forced him to withdraw from active duty with Maxey's Company. But in 1863 Jeff took a beating from Turner Edmundson, a large man who was a former mayor of Paris. After recuperating enough to wield a shotgun, Jeff blasted Edmundson fatally in downtown Paris. The beating he had taken helped him win acquittal, and Jeff soon left town to join John on the range.[14]

As a Confederate beef supplier, John Chisum agreed to accept a delivery price of forty dollars per head, with designated delivery points in the Trans-Mississippi Department. Late in 1861 Chisum led a herd of 750 cattle toward Vicksburg, a major Confederate strongpoint on the east bank of the Mississippi River. There were seven other riders, along with Giles Chisum, a nineteen-year-old black man who worked as cook and drove the supply wagon. John Chisum crossed the Red River at Colbert's Ferry and followed the north side of the Red River, which angled down to Shreveport. From there the herd was driven due east across northern Louisiana. The longhorns were nervous, spooked by the forests and marshy terrain, and there was a stampede on the approach to Vicksburg. Once the herd was back together, two days were spent shoving the cattle onto barges and ferrying them across the mile-wide Mississippi. And after Chisum paid off his crew, several men joined the Confederate Army.[15]

Chisum returned to Denton County with only two cowboys and the cook, Giles Chisum, in addition to a carpenter and a young black boy they encountered on the trail. When he arrived at his ranch, Chisum found that conditions had deteriorated in his absence. He had agreed to tend cattle for half a dozen neighbors, and he wrote to one of them on March 7, 1862:

> I got back from Vicksburg a few days since. I find the Prairies
> all burnt off and we have had no rain hear [sic] since last

spring . . . All my hands are gon [sic], all my horses are gon. I
am left behind in charge of 6 other stock besides own.[16]

The U.S. Army had been active in Texas during the 1850s,
manning numerous outposts and sending forth cavalry patrols
and pursuit parties. But federal troops were withdrawn early in
1861, with the outbreak of the Civil War. Horseback warriors,
Comanches, and Kiowas—the feared "Wild Tribes"—pushed
the Texas frontier back during the next several years, causing
the abandonment of many ranches.

John Chisum, however, could afford to buy new horses
and hire new men and even buy new parcels of land. At forty
dollars per head, he returned to Texas with more than $30,000
in Confederate currency, and he put that money to work. By
contrast, Jesse Driskill, a cattleman from the Austin area, also
was appointed beef supplier for the Confederate Army. Driskill dutifully delivered cattle to CSA troops throughout the war,
but he was caught with a great deal of worthless Confederate
currency at the end of the war. John Chisum, on the other hand,
delivered three more herds to Confederate forces, and in each
instance, he used the cash to purchase more cattle or horses or
land. As a result, Chisum held little valueless currency after the
Confederate surrender.[17]

There were more than 92,000 Texas men between the ages of
seventeen and forty-five in the Census of 1860, and during the
war 70,000 Texans served the Confederacy. Many volunteered
with Home Guard militia units, but manpower was scarce in
Texas throughout the war. Somehow Chisum scraped up crews
for more trail drives. Again heading east along the Red River
Valley, Chisum took a herd across the southeast corner of Indian Territory and angled northeast to Little Rock. Chisum made
two drives to Little Rock, along with one to Shreveport.[18]

These drives eastward through forested country were difficult to control and hard on cattle. Insects plagued the animals,

while cockle burrs and mud balls accumulated on their tails. Chisum "became convinced that little could be made from driving on account of the insects, dense woods, and broad rivers."[19] Chisum began to look westward, a natural direction for a man with his pioneer instincts.

He was further influenced by the course of the Civil War. Early in July 1863, Vicksburg surrendered to the federal army of General Ulysses Grant, and General Robert E. Lee suffered a crushing defeat at the three-day Battle of Gettysburg. With the fall of Vicksburg, the entire Mississippi River was in the hands of Union troops, while Texas, Arkansas, and Louisiana were separated from the other Confederate states. Indeed, Arkansas soon was seized by federal troops and was readmitted to the Union, while Louisiana was readmitted in 1864. The end was dearly in sight for John Chisum's career as a Confederate beef supplier.

Chapter Three
In Search of Open Range

"He was never afraid of anything or anybody. . . ."
—**Mrs. J. Smith Lea**

Legendary cattleman Charles Goodnight stated, " He was a great trail man." Goodnight worked closely with John Chisum for several years during the 1860s and 1870s. "No one had any advantage of him as an old-fashioned cowman, and he was the best counter I ever knew."[1]

During nearly a decade as a rancher in Denton County, John Chisum had become an expert at handling cattle. He was a fine rider and was skilled with rope and branding iron—and pocket knife, in fashioning his unique earmark. He had led numerous trail drives, and he would continue to drive cattle or horse herds into his fifties.

In 1863 Chisum was still in his thirties. He was five-eight, with a lean, wiry physique and the deep tan of a man who spent most of his time in Texas sun. Chisum was dark-haired and gray-eyed, and he sported a large moustache. In conversation Chisum chuckled good-naturedly and often laughed raucously. "It was a man's laugh, loud and deep," described a young lady after meeting him for the first time, "a laugh not merely from the diaphragm, but one that implied the whole body."[2]

His humor often was self-deprecating, and he was even-tempered, refusing to show anger. Chisum seemed to encourage people to underestimate him. As one acquaintance observed, Chisum "was rather inclined to make people believe that he was not so bright. He was never afraid of anything or anybody, and if he ever got mad, no one ever knew it . . ."[3] Except that sometimes the laughter became a bit cold, and his jokes could be tinged with sarcasm.

With settlers moving into the prime farm country that Chisum was using as open range, and following the devastating Confederate defeats at Vicksburg and Gettysburg in July 1863, the ambitious rancher decided to begin locating cattle on range he had scouted a few years earlier. In 1856 Chisum and a cowboy in his employ, Felix McKittrick, rode along the military road between Fort Belknap and Fort Mason, headquarters of the new Second Cavalry Regiment.[4] A cavalry outpost, Camp Colorado, was established in July 1856 near Mukewater Creek in what is today Coleman County, although a year later the station was relocated more than twenty miles to the north.

Coleman County was created in 1858, but organization of a county government took several more years. The first Anglo community in Coleman County was Camp Colorado, which was abandoned by federal troops in 1861. The first non-military community was Trickham on Mukewater Creek in the southeast corner of the county. There was a log store, owned by Bill Franks, and a few cabins. The little store was a gathering place, and practical jokes led to the hamlet being labeled "Trick-em," which eventually became

A marker fashioned locally in Trickham recounts: "Trickham, Texas, was on the military road from Ft. Mason to Ft. Belknap in the 1850s. Here camped Johnston, Van Dorn, Lee, and other army men. Here John Chisum gathered herds of cattle in the 1860s. This was the last town on the Western Trail to Kansas." *Photo by the author.*

Trickham.

Late in 1863 John Chisum, with Felix McKittrick and about ten other drovers, led 1,500 head of cattle from Denton County southwest toward Coleman County. A cook wagon was pulled by a big team of mules and driven by the black cook, Giles Chisum. Five ox-drawn wagons carried supplies and equipment. The trail was roughly 240 miles and took about three weeks, with a crossing of the Brazos River at Fort Belknap. Chisum entered Coleman County at Trickham, the only settlement in the county. Mukewater Creek ran north-to-south past Trickham. About six miles below Trickham Mukewater Creek flowed into the Colorado River, the southern boundary of the county. A few miles west of Mukewater Creek was another north-to-south stream, Home Creek, where Chisum decided to locate his ranch headquarters. He set his men to erecting a few dugout cabins and corrals "in a monte of pecan trees," and later other corrals were built at other points across the range he pre-empted in southern Coleman County. "The ranch house was built of pecan logs," described a Chisum cowboy, "with three large rooms, and was so sturdy that it would serve for a good fort in time of trouble."[5]

The terrain was rolling prairie with occasional tall hills, where cattle could find shelter from winter storms. Along the Colorado River and lesser streams were scattered cottonwood trees, along with elm and pecan trees. Chisum's cattle made up the first substantial herd in the region, and his Jinglebobs feasted on a buffet of mesquite grass and buffalo grass, as well as grama, needle, and spear grasses.

Leaving a few men at Home Creek to improve the primitive headquarters complex and to keep an eye on the cattle, Chisum returned to Denton County for another herd. There were drives to Coleman County throughout 1864 and into 1865. A young cowboy named Ike Fridge, who had worked for Chisum since he was fourteen, rode on one of the first drives from the Denton County ranch. "Ideal weather and good grazing for the herds made this a wonderful trip," he reminisced. "Crossing through country that was a treat to the eye, and fording beautiful streams at intervals, we had a fine time on the drive." By 1865 there were 18,000 Jinglebobs grazing across southern Coleman County, and into Concho and Runnels counties to the west.[6]

In 1864 Chisum's ten-year partnership with Stephen K. Fowler expired. Fowler's capital investment had made it possible for Chisum to enter the cattle business on a sizeable scale. But after a decade as a pioneer rancher, Chisum was well-established in the range cattle business and he wanted to be an independent operator. Chisum informed Fowler that he did not want to renew their partnership agreement. He proposed to either buy or sell their mutual interests, adding pointedly that "he would thereafter run only Chisum's cattle, or he would withdraw from the business of stock raising altogether."[7]

Chisum probably was bluffing with the latter remark. He had enjoyed great success at accumulating vast numbers of cattle, and he was poised to find profitable markets for his herds. And, as he must have expected, Stephen Fowler did not challenge Chisum's bargaining point. Fowler was no cattleman, and he agreed to sell out to Chisum. With his forty-dollar-per-head Confederate beef prices, Chisum had speculated in parcels of land, mostly in Denton County. Fowler accepted the land as payment from his longtime partner, and John Chisum now was totally independent as a rancher. He could seek "a free and unlimited range" in order to build up an unlimited herd.[8]

Chisum's herd of longhorns scattered widely over his new range, and when a roundup was needed meal conditions were primitive, since the chuck wagon had not yet been invented. "We started on a cow hunt with an outfit of twenty men, with three horses to the man, and two pack horses," remembered a Chisum cowboy. "We had no skillets for frying, but each man had a tin for his coffee, and a rusty bread pan was tied on a pack horse. Our bread was made of flour, cold water, salt and soda. Each man cut him a green stick for his cooking. We trimmed the bark off, took the dough and rolled it around the stick and cooked it over the fire. Our meat was also cooked over the fire on the green boughs."[9]

In order to avoid hauling in supplies from Fort Worth, about 180 miles to the northeast, or from Austin, almost as far it to the southeast, Chisum acquired the store of Bill Franks at Trickham. Franks continue to work in the store, and Chisum sometimes sent him to an Austin bank to deposit money from a cattle sale, or to bring back gold or silver coin to meet a payroll. Emory Peter, a cowboy with a crippled hand, was assigned to run the store, and he also began to function as Chisum's bookkeeper.[10] Chisum, of course, had amassed considerable experience as a store clerk in his younger years. His ranch supply store also was patronized by settlers, and he maintained ownership of the business for years after he moved to New Mexico. Chisum's store, "about 20 x 40 feet, had port holes for use in repulsing Indians, and was surrounded by a high picket fence," according to Ike Fridge.[11]

During this period Pitser Chisum began working for his older brother. Following Civil War service Pitser, still single, joined John's ranching enterprise. He proved to be a capable trail boss and, later, he would serve as ranch manager in New Mexico. By 1865 Jeff Chisum, who had killed a man in Paris in 1863, became part of the Home Creek ranch team, accompanying one of the trail drives to Coleman County. But Jeff's health clearly was impaired by his epileptic condition, and his physical fragility was a serious concern.

Although the Civil War ended in 1865, the federal troops that were stationed in post-war Texas represented an occupation force in the eastern third of the state. These troops tried to enforce Reconstruction policies, rather than provide protection to frontier settlers. The forts that had been abandoned in 1861 remained unoccupied until 1867, and Comanche and Kiowa war parties pushed the Texas frontier back 100 miles during those years. Four out of five ranches were abandoned in the frontier counties, as settlers were killed and livestock was stolen. Indeed, in Denton County in 1862 John Chisum lost a horse herd to Comanche raiders, who drove the animals across the Red River into Indian Territory. After returning from a cattle drive to Vicksburg, he reported that his grass had been burned and "all my horses are gon." It was told that Oliver Loving, who ranched farther west in Palo Pinto County, also had lost horses, and that he enlisted Chisum in a successful effort to slip into Indian Territory and recover their horses.[12]

When Chisum move to Coleman County his ranching operation was even more exposed than in Denton County. Not long after he relocated, Chisum began to be harassed by Comanche raiders. Furthermore, Confederate deserters began to take refuge on the edge of the Texas frontier. These outlaws "commenced stealing everything they could find, and as cattle were numerous . . . the thieves turned their attention to stock, and ran them off or slaughtered them for their hides, which were then worth more than the carcass."[13]

Pioneer cattleman Oliver Loving found a kindred spirit in John Chisum. *Author's collection.*

Plagued by rustlers and horseback warriors, Chisum found himself thinking about another move west. This inclination soon was influenced by two other noted pioneers of the range cattle industry. Oliver Loving was in his fifties, twenty-two years older than John Chisum. When Chisum was in his early twenties, Loving migrated from his native Kentucky to Lamar County in the Texas Republic. Perhaps he met John Chisum in 1845, but Loving soon moved to Collin County, where he farmed and freighted and raised cattle. In 1855 he began ranching in Palo Pinto County, and in 1858 Loving sent a cattle herd to the Chicago stockyards, making a profit of thirty-six dollars per head. Like John Chisum, Loving supplied beef to the Confederate Army during the Civil War.

Loving began working with another Palo Pinto County rancher, Charles Goodnight. Born in Illinois in 1836, Goodnight was twenty-four years younger than Oliver Loving and twelve years junior to John Chisum. At ten Goodnight moved with his family to Texas, and by the time he was twenty Goodnight was running cattle in Palo Pinto County. While serving as a Texas Ranger he learned to take precautions against war parties—precautions he would carefully employ on his trail drives. By the end of the Civil War there were millions of longhorns running wild in Texas, but they were worth very little in the Lone Star State. Goodnight, however, learned of a new Indian reservation at Fort Sumner in eastern New Mexico that needed large numbers of cattle to feed more than 8,000 Navajo and Mescalero Apache men, women, and children.

In the spring of 1866 Goodnight prepared for a long trail drive across harsh country. To feed his range crew he had a military wagon rebuilt with tough bois d'arc wood and iron axles. Goodnight designed a chuck box, covered by a hinged lid that would be lowered onto a swinging leg to form the cook's worktable.[14] Goodnight's chuck wagon rapidly became an iconic feature of the range cattle industry, and it soon was adapted by John Chisum, who would launch one trail drive after another in ensuing years.

Goodnight invited Oliver Loving to join him with a combined herd. After hearing Goodnight's plan, the aging but adventurous cattleman agreed to set out for New Mexico along a new trail he and Goodnight would blaze. Also in 1866, other Texas cattlemen were heading north with herds of longhorns, hoping to intersect with a railroad in Missouri that would ship their cattle to markets in the northeast. Few of those drives were successful in reaching a railroad, but in 1867 the Chisholm Trail was opened, shifting the journey to the west and to Abilene, Kansas. The trail

Jesse Chisholm blazed the Chisholm Trail to Abilene, Kansas, in 1867, creating a permanent confusion with cattle king John Chisum. *Author collection.*

was named after an old Indian trader, Jesse Chisholm, and because of similar pronunciations the blazing of this most famous of cattle routes often would be credited to John Chisum. For nearly two decades Kansas railheads of the Chisholm Trail and, a few years later, the Great Western Trail, would handle millions of cattle from Texas. But John Chisum saw his future not to the north but to the west, and soon he joined Charles Goodnight and Oliver Loving.

Goodnight and Loving put together a mixed herd of 2,000 steers, cows, and calves, and a crew of eighteen drovers. The outfit departed on an epic journey in June 1866. Goodnight led the way south and west, arriving at the Concho River near the site of a major new outpost—Fort Concho—which would be built the next year. The herd was trailed just above the range which John Chisum had appropriated for his vast herd. The trail drive followed the Middle Concho River as far as it ran, and from there stretched a waterless trek of ninety miles west to the Pecos River. The Pecos has steep embankments that are several feet tall, but Horsehead Crossing would become the customary ford for the Goodnight–Loving Trail. From Horsehead Crossing the Pecos turned north into New Mexico.

"At that time the Pecos was the most desolate country that I had ever explored," recounted Goodnight. "The river was full of fish, but besides the fish there was scarcely a living thing, not even wolves or birds." Except, that is, for rattlesnakes. "They were there by the hundreds, and still are."[15]

The drive followed the Pecos northward. Now there was plenty of water, although the quality of Pecos water is strongly alkaline. And there was a great deal of quicksand alongside the river. When cattle bogged down in quicksand, the cowboys struggled–often in vain–to free them.

"The Pecos–the graveyard of the cowman's hopes," recalled Goodnight with vehemence. "I hated it!"[16] But alongside this treacherous river John Chisum soon built the West's greatest open range ranch.

When Goodnight and Loving reached Fort Sumner, they found the reservation Indians on the verge of starvation. They sold their steers, from two-year-olds and older, "for the high price of eight cents a pounds on foot." They were paid $12,000 in gold, and they still held more than 700 cows and calves. The partners decided that Loving and the crew would drive the remaining cattle northward into Colorado's mining country, while Goodnight would return to Texas to put together another herd. In northern Colorado Loving sold his herd to another early cattle king, John Wesley Iliff. The partners had received a dazzling bonanza, while opening a major cattle trail out of Texas. Goodnight promptly backtracked the Goodnight-Loving Trail with three cowboys and a pack mule carrying supplies and $12,000 in gold.[17]

Goodnight and his companions made the return trip to Texas in seventeen days. Another crew was hired, another herd was gathered, and a second drive launched. After about forty days Goodnight and Loving reunited at Bosque Grande, roughly forty miles south of Fort Sumner and the Bosque Redondo Reservation. Goodnight and Loving established a winter camp at Bosque Grande, building dugouts on the east side of the Pecos River. Through the winter the partners made regular deliveries to Fort Sumner and, occasionally, to other buyers.

News of the success of Goodnight and Loving had spread through cow country, and a few Texas ranchers tried to drive herds up the trail. As John Chisum digested the new developments, including beef contracts in New Mexico Territory, he decided to send his brother Pitser to scout out the New Mexico ranges. Pitser rode into New Mexico up the Pecos River in 1866 and took his time inspecting grazing sections. Jeff Chisum may have ridden along, because the frail epileptic died in 1866 in Puerto de Luna, about thirty-five miles northwest of Fort Sumner. A beating in a local saloon contributed to his death at thirty-seven. Two years later Chisum learned that his older sister, Nancy Bourland, had died at forty-six. Nancy and her husband Benjamin were the parents of eleven children, and their youngest was only two when she lost her mother.[18]

By 1867 Goodnight and Loving had collected another herd of Texas longhorns and commenced the third drive to New Mexico within a year. But Comanches had detected the activity along the new trail, and there was Indian trouble. Goodnight saw that his men were well-armed and he proceeded cautiously. Loving, with scout Bill Wilson, pushed ahead to make a deal for the cattle at Fort Sumner. Goodnight urged Loving to travel only at night, but Loving soon impatiently proceeded forward in daylight. Jumped by a war party, Loving suffered two wounds, including a shattered wrist. He dug into the em-

bankment at what would become known as Loving's Bend of
the Pecos. Wilson was sent back to the herd for help, while the
injured Loving held off the warriors for two days. On the third
night Loving escaped upriver, and several days later he was
found by Mexicans and transported north by wagon. At Fort
Sumner the post surgeon realized that gangrene had infected
his arm, which had to be amputated. When Goodnight reached
the outpost, the weakened Loving extracted a promise to carry him back to Texas for burial. Loving died on September 25,
1867, and his remains were taken in a wagon by Goodnight and
an escort of cowboys for final interment by Masonic services in
Weatherford. (This incident was dramatized and embellished
by Larry McMurtry in his Pulitzer Prize-winning novel, *Lonesome Dove*.)

Meanwhile, Pitser Chisum returned to Texas "and reported
to his brother that the country watered by the Pecos River presented a good field for cattle raising, there being not then a hoof
of stock on it from Fort Sumner down to Horsehead Crossing,
Texas."[19]

John Chisum was strongly attracted to this empty new
range, but before moving his entire operation out of Texas he
needed to see the country for himself. And if Chisum was riding to New Mexico, he might as well lead a cattle herd up the
new trail to Fort Sumner. He always had been good at negotiat-
ing the sale and purchase of livestock herds, and he was confident that he could be as successful as anyone at finding buyers
in New Mexico Territory.

Chapter Four
On to New Mexico

*"The ranchers were nomadic, casting
themselves out on the great sea of grass."*

—T.R. Fehrenbach, Texas historian

During the spring of 1867 John Chisum rounded up a herd of more than 900 steers from his Coleman County range. He intended to shove this herd up the Goodnight-Loving Trail, despite the threat of war parties and difficult conditions of the route. Chisum confidently reasoned that if others had driven herds successfully up this trail, he was tough enough and skilled enough to do the same.

Chisum led his herd to the headwaters of the Middle Concho River, then set out across ninety waterless miles toward the Pecos. The cattle plodded along with swollen tongues until, a few miles from Horsehead Crossing, they began to smell water. Although Chisum tried to head off the herd, the suffering beasts stampeded straight to the river, scrambling down Horsehead Crossing to the reddish, brackish water.[1]

The twisting, steep-banked Pecos offered few places to cross or even to water a herd safely. There were mountains to the west, and eastern-flowing tributaries brought fresh water into the west bank. But to the east of the Pecos the land was flat and there were no tributaries. Goodnight had chosen to drive his herd along the east bank of the river to avoid difficult crossings, although the poor quality of the water cost him dead livestock. (Horsehead Crossing got its name from the skulls of dead hors-

The Frontiers of John Chisum

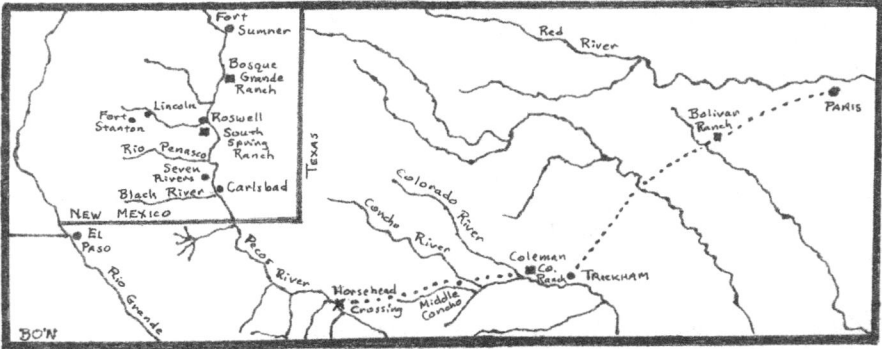

Map–Frontiers of John Chisum

es.) Chisum chose to proceed up the west bank to provide fresh water for his cattle, despite the necessity of making several crossings. Therefore the Goodnight-Loving Trail in New Mexico proceeded north toward Fort Sumner along the east bank of the Pecos, while the "Chisum Trail" moved north largely along the west bank.[2]

Chisum halted his herd at Bosque Grande, which had become a rendezvous point during the past couple of years. Bosque Grande meant Big Grove, referring to a large grove of cottonwood trees beside the Pecos. Just to the west is Bosque Grande Mesa, a long plateau. Chisum arrived at Bosque Grande with his cattle in August 1867. With plenty of wood for winter fuel, he established a cow camp at Bosque Grande and released his herd onto the vacant range on the east side of the Pecos. The east bank of the Pecos marked the beginning of the Llano Estacado, the vast Staked Plains, home of buffalo and the Comanche. The cattle herd wintered successfully, while Chisum sought a buyer.[3]

James Patterson was an agent for Stadtahr & Co. of New York, which held the beef contract for Fort Sumner and the Bosque Redondo Reservation. Indeed, Patterson had handled the sale of the first Goodnight-Loving herd that arrived in New

Mexico in 1866, and he had opened a trading post at Bosque Grande. Chisum agreed to sell his herd to Patterson for $28,000 payable by drafts on the firm of Stadtahr & Co. But with regrettable timing, Stadtahr & Co. failed and Chisum's drafts were worthless. "The loss was a heavy one for Uncle John," related Lily Klasner, who heard all about his life from a garrulous Chisum, "but he knew how to take misfortune philosophically."[4]

One reason for Chisum's equanimity was the success of the sale of his herd–except for the complete loss of payment–and the prospect of such sales in the future. Cattle were available in Texas in profusion, and with the failure of Stadtahr & Co., James Patterson procured a government contract to supply 7,000 head of cattle for the reservation Indians. Every animal "that would make meat" was to be counted at the following rates: "cow and calf, $16.00; yearlings, $6.00; two-year-olds, $9.00; threes and dry cows, $18.00; and fours and up, $25.00."[5]

Chisum now realized that he could build a cattle operation of truly gigantic proportions. He had access to an enormous, vacant range, along with the prospects of multiple contracts. Leaving Pitser in charge at the Bosque Grande headquarters camp, Chisum hurried back to Texas in the spring of 1868 to begin gathering and delivering herds. There was good rain that spring and Chisum led

John Chisum, from a closeup of the statue by Robert Temple Summers in Roswell. *Photo by the author.*

the trek to Horsehead Crossing with the cattle in good shape. He delivered the herd to Bosque Grande, then rode back to Texas for more cattle.

This hectic pace was about to accelerate when Chisum joined forces with another giant of the frontier range cattle industry. With Oliver Loving dead, Charles Goodnight needed a new partner in order to gather and deliver thousands of head of cattle to government contractors and to buyers in Colorado and Wyoming. John Chisum, eager to provide as many cattle as possible, agreed to a partnership with Charles Goodnight. "Goodnight contracted to receive Chisum's drives at Bosque Grande on a fifty-fifty basis," explained J. Evetts Haley, "allowing him a dollar a head extra for his risks on the trail from Texas."[6]

Goodnight delivered a herd to John Wesley Iliff in northeastern Colorado when, according to his calculations, John Chisum was setting out with the first herd of their new partnership. Goodnight led his men in a hard ride toward New Mexico, arriving at Bosque Grande just in time to meet Chisum. Goodnight and his men took over the cattle and headed them toward Colorado.

The next few years Goodnight and Chisum repeated their herd exchange at Bosque Grande, over and over, as fast as they could buy and sell and drive their herds. "Bosque Grande got to be a sort of trading point," wrote Goodnight. "Chisum and I bought there and other

CHARLES GOODNIGHT.

Charles Goodnight had an informal but productive partnership with John Chisum. *Author's collection.*

buyers began to come. Many herds changed hands there and went on north." Goodnight told his biographer how "day in and night out through 1868 and 1869, he drove himself relentlessly up and down the trail from southern New Mexico to Wyoming." Goodnight related that "his longest stay in any one place was a four days' pause in Denver."[7]

But if Goodnight's schedule was relentless, so was Chisum's, who was driving herd after herd from Texas to Bosque Grande. Chisum began to have Pitser—whom he called "P.M."—meet him at Horsehead Crossing. Pitser could lead the herd the last couple of hundred miles to Bosque Grande, while John had a much shorter ride back to collect and start another herd.

In June 1869 Chisum turned over to P.M. a herd of 1,165 steers which he had bought from a rancher on the South Concho River. He paid $20 a head, but the contract called for a sale price of $35 a head. Starting from the South Concho, he made it safely to Horsehead Crossing and delivered the herd to P.M. There had been an Apache outbreak, and when Pitser encountered a company of soldiers he asked for an escort. His request was denied. On June 12, 1869, Pitser camped on the Black River, east of the Guadalupe Mountains. That night a large war party struck the herd and an exchange of fire broke out.

"In this fight several Indians were killed," related John Chisum to a newspaper reporter, "and one cowboy was wounded." The warriors stampeded the cattle and escaped to the mountains with the entire herd. As usual, Chisum shrugged off the loss. Several weeks later he brought more cattle to Pitser at Horsehead Crossing. Chisum smiled at his brother and pointed at the herd. "Well, P.M., here's another herd; try her again."[8]

A year later, during a roundup at Coleman County ranch in Texas, Comanche raiders swooped down and raced away with the remuda. Leaving half a dozen men at the ranch, Chisum took a crew and rode to San Antonio to purchase another cavvy of horses. He returned to the ranch without incident and began organizing a cattle drive to New Mexico. But the day before departing for the trail, Comanches struck again. "After a short skirmish the red skins succeeded in getting away with all of our horses except five head," related cowboy Ike Fridge. Chisum picked Fridge, a cowboy named Smith," and a half-breed Indian" to accompany him back to San Antonio for more saddle stock. Chisum rode a mule, which left a couple of horses for the ranch crew.[9]

Chisum often chose to ride a mule, for a smoother, steadier gait. Mules are not as jumpy as horses and exhibit more stamina, probably because they do not waste as much nervous energy. Whether on a horse or mule, Chisum usually wrapped a gun belt around his saddle horn, with the revolver handle available to his right hand. It is often reported that Chisum never wore a gun. He may not have *worn* a gun rig, but he carried one on his saddle, and when he drove a buggy he brought along a Winchester.[10]

In the spring of 1872 another Chisum crew was placed on foot by another war party. Chisum sent several thousand cattle from Texas in two bunches with separate crews. The first trail herd had trouble at Horsehead Crossing and one cowboy was killed before the herd was able to push ahead to the north. A few days later the second herd passed by Horsehead Crossing without incident. But, camped at Loving's Bend–where Oliver Loving had been fatally wounded in 1867–the Jinglebob outfit was struck at night. Four night hawks were guarding the cattle, but the warriors galloped away into the darkness with the remuda. The only saddle horses left were the four mounts of the night hawks.

For the rest of the drive the trail boss used four mounted men "to point the herd and for flankers, the rest of the boys driving on foot and helping to keep the bunch moving," according to Ike Fridge. "We made it to the ranch in fifteen days with the entire herd except possibly a few which the boys had to use their 'Colts' on to keep from being run down and gored by the long keen horns known only to the 'Texas Longhorn' and other kindred breeds."[11]

Ike Fridge was wounded during a night attack by Comanches while helping to bring a herd of saddle horses back to Texas for another trail drive to Bosque Grande. Camp was made just twelve miles west of Fort Concho and a day's ride to Chisum range. But that night Comanche raiders struck the camp. While some of the raiders rode off into the darkness with as many horses as they could stampede, other warriors pinned down the cowboys around the chuck wagon. A bullet struck a metal wagon tire and shattered, and a sliver of metal struck Fridge in the head. His friends pulled out the piece of shrapnel, but one cowboy was killed and another wounded. The next day the crew buried their dead friends in the post cemetery, while the wounded cowboy was taken to the Fort Concho hospital.[12]

Fridge described a typical *remuda* used by Chisum crews. "We had a saddle *remuda* of one hundred head of horses, among which was every kind of cayuse you could wish for. There were horses that were trained for roping and holding, for cutting herd; and all the tricks known to the typical cow horse of the Southwest were in the bunch. Among these horses were to be found tough buckers, easy saddlers and a few good racers to furnish amusement at the proper time."[13]

John Chisum stayed busy buying saddle horses as well as cattle. Because of constant raids by Comanches and Kiowas, he found many ranchers eager to sell their livestock cheaply. After finally completing a trail drive, Chisum like to break out a keg of whiskey. He always enjoyed celebrations. Charles Goodnight, on the other hand, was a forceful disciplinarian, imposing three rules on his riders: no drinking, no gambling, and no fighting. But he was willing to overlook Chisum's intemperate side because of the great success the partners were producing. However, after Chisum later lost a herd to a war party and hastily gathered a replacement herd "without regard to make or brand," Goodnight refused to accept livestock of such questionable ownership. Biographer Haley reported that "the genial Chisum took no offense, though Goodnight took him to task and then went his way."[14]

But Chisum overlooked Goodnight's occasional displeasure, while the big, bearded Goodnight tolerated Chisum's easygoing discretions. Small wonder that the partners exercised a little tolerance with each other. During a three-year period Chisum delivered 15,000 to 16,000 head of cattle to Goodnight in New Mexico. Profits were at least $35,000. Goodnight put his share of the proceeds into a Colorado ranch he was developing above Pueblo, while Chisum used his money to stock his Bosque Grande range with cows and heifers. Indeed, any unsold cattle from the herds he had delivered had been turned onto Chisum's range. John Chisum already had established New Mexico's first truly large ranch, and he intended to make it larger.[15]

Deciding to transfer his herds from Texas to New Mexico, Chisum established his new headquarters at Bosque Grande. He bought James Patterson's trading post and residence. As at Trickham, he now had a ranch supply store and mercantile. Chisum erected corrals at the thicket, along with a few additional structures. He assigned half a dozen riders to keep buffalo off the vast range east of the Pecos. "During the cold 'northers' the buffalo would drift in by the thousand," explained one of the cowboys, "and we had to turn them from the choice range to save it for the cattle."[16]

Chisum began to establish cow camps at strategic points on the range he used, including one at Carlsbad Springs on the lower Pecos, more than 120 miles south of Bosque Grande. One line camp featured a dugout in a little draw with the roof of poles and dirt. "The door was made of box lids and rawhide strings," while the chimney was cut into the bank "and topped off with large rocks." Two cowboys named Goodwin and Walker were wintering in the line cabin when they were attacked by an Apache war party. When the warriors began trying to dig through the roof, the cowboys made a break. Although Walker was shot down Goodwin managed to escape, only to be killed in another skirmish a month later.[17]

Jim Jones cowboyed for John Chisum during the mid-1870s. He fought in the five-day Battle of Lincoln, and later ran his own ranch west of Seven Rivers until his death in 1930. In 1927 he was interviewed by the industrious cow country historian J. Evetts Haley. Jones related that Chisum maintained twenty line camps across his Pecos Valley range, from above the Texas border almost to Fort Sumner. Each winter two cowboys were stationed at each line camp. Jones was assigned to the northernmost camp, halfway between Fort Sumner and Bosque Grande. Every day Jones rode west for ten miles and checked cattle until he encountered another Chisum cowboy riding from the west. Jones would take another route back to the camp, completing a twenty-mile circuit. His line camp partner rode east for ten miles until he met a cowboy coming from the east.

The camp partners had only one horse each during the winters, keeping the two mounts at night in one room of their two-room dugout to prevent theft by Indians. The horses were fed corn and grama grass hay brought in from Las Vegas by wagons. Chisum kept the line camps stocked with provisions: fresh beef, bacon, potatoes, *frijoles*, syrup for biscuits, sugar, and coffee.

In the spring Chisum placed about 3,000 cows in each of twenty herds, with one bull for every twenty cows. Only one roundup was held each year, throughout the month of September. The roundup commenced in the south, with crews moving cattle on both sides of the Pecos. Each roundup cowboy was allotted five horses. Chisum bought his horses in Texas. All geldings, most of these mounts were Spanish stock. "I don't think Chisum could be beat as a cowman," remarked Jones, "but he seemed to want the Pecos country all to himself."[18]

On July 19, 1873, a band of warriors galloped up to the corral beside the Chisum store on the Bosque Grande. The raiders had targeted a herd "of 125 picked saddle horses," which were defended by gunfire from Chisum men inside the store. Although several warriors were hit, the raiders escaped with the horses. Two days later, at a roundup camp directed by Pitser Chisum, another raiding party stole forty mounts. That same day Felix McKittrick and his roundup crew were struck by perhaps the same band of warriors. A furious firefight erupted, with one cowboy killed and eighty horses stampeded. As customary, the warriors carried off any casualties they had suffered. One of Chisum's line riders, Newt Huggins, was killed and scalped during this troubled period. In the fall of 1873 another raiding party stole sixty horses from a branding camp at Eighteen-Mile Bend on the Pecos, and cowboy Jack Holt was killed. While the principal objective of war parties was to steal horses, they also killed "many thousands of cattle, the bones of which at the present time give a bovine graveyard appearance to many of the watering places on the old Chisum Ranch."[19]

T.R. Fehrenbach, in *Lone Star*, his epic history of Texas and Texans, wrote insightfully about frontier ranchers. "Cowmen came from everywhere, not only because the beef business was booming, but because something in its way of life called strongly to certain breeds of men . . . A Charles Goodnight could move early onto the far edge of nowhere, and hold his new range against all comers. Some men could not."[20]

The same certainly could have been said about John Chisum. Chisum indeed had moved onto the edge of nowhere and held his new range against all comers. He had pioneered three new ranges, and he had held his trio of frontier ranches against Comanche and Apache warriors, against thieving rustlers, and against cruel conditions of weather and terrain. He faced every challenge, every threat fearlessly and with calm tenacity.

Chisum and Goodnight discontinued their partnership by 1871. Within a few years Goodnight returned to Texas, opening a ranch in Palo Duro Canyon as soon as the U.S. Army drove Comanches from this longtime winter sanctuary. Goodnight acquired a partner, John Adair, and within a decade more than 100,000 JAs cattle grazed on over 1,335,000 acres. But John Chisum already had found his dream ranch, and he resolutely determined to hold it against all comers.

As Chisum's herds expanded far to the south, he decided to move his ranch headquarters from Bosque Grande to a site closer to the center of his lengthy Pecos Valley range. And once again James Patterson had an attractive location and he was willing to sell.

Chapter Five
Rustlers and Other Cow Country Outlaws

"He killed the boy. Why not hang him?"
—John Chisum

The South Spring River is an artesian stream that bubbles out of the ground a few miles south of Roswell. If flows eastward toward the Pecos River, which runs north-to-south a little to the east of Roswell. The stream is so short—only a few miles from its source to the Pecos—that it sometimes was called South Spring Creek. But fresh water gushed abundantly from the South Spring, and John Chisum, raised a farm boy, immediately recognized the agricultural possibilities of irrigation in an arid land.

James Patterson owned a forty-acre parcel that was bisected by the South Spring River. The most substantial structure on the property was an eight-room, flat-roofed adobe that stood on the south bank of the South Spring River. The rooms, including a long bunk room for cowboys, opened onto a patio about twenty feet square. A horse corral was attached to the west side of the building, which was called the "Square House."[1] The Square House was a major step up from the log cabin at Bosque Grande for the passersby that Chisum had learned to expect—and to enjoy.

In December 1874 John Chisum acquired from James Patterson the forty-acre property and the Square House, along with household and kitchen furnishings, farm implements, and two yoke of oxen. There also was a small house located beside a long

The Square House

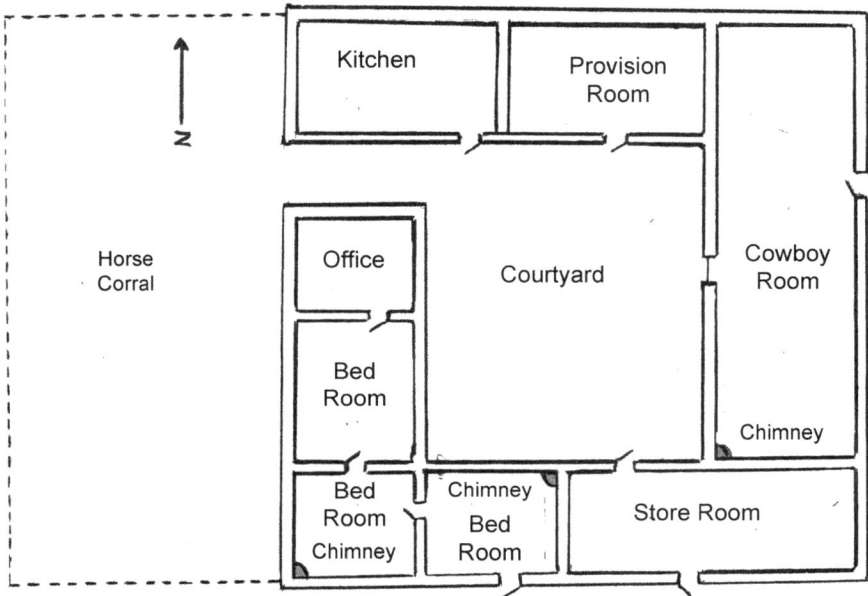

The Square House of South Spring.
Adapted from a drawing by Will Chisum on file at the Haley Memorial Library.

acequia (irrigation ditch). Patterson accepted the transaction "in consideration of the sum of twenty-five hundred dollars to be paid in cattle." Chisum provided twenty-four hundred head of cattle to pay off Patterson.[2]

The Bosque Redondo Reservation, where John Chisum had supplied rich beef contracts during his first years in New Mexico, was closed in 1868. In 1863 the U.S. Army had forcibly removed 10,000 Navajos from their traditional homelands and moved the tribe 450 miles to the southwest to the Bosque Redondo. On this Navajo version of the Trail of Tears great numbers died, and within five years at Bosque Redondo the Navajo had lost twenty percent of their people. The government relented and escorted the surviving Navajos back to their homeland. Fort Sumner, which had been built to support the reservation, was abandoned by the army. The deserted post buildings were appropriated by civilians, and the community of Fort Sumner

Head of the South Spring River a few miles from ranch headquarters. JEH I.F 15.9.
Courtesy Haley Memorial Library

developed rapidly.

About 500 Mescalero Apaches also had been confined at Bosque Redondo. The Mescaleros now were moved more than 150 miles southwest, to a mountain reservation just south of Fort Stanton, which had been established in 1855. The Mescalero reservation was only seventy miles west of South Spring, and Chisum predictably began filling beef contracts to Fort Stanton, as well as to the large supply depot at Fort Union in northeastern New Mexico.

Fort Stanton was only ten miles west of Lincoln, the seat of Lincoln County. Lincoln was a small adobe town with a single winding street, which paralleled the Rio Bonito, just north of the little community. Lincoln County was the largest county in the United States, encompassing a sparsely settled region of 27,000 square miles. Comprising almost all of the southeastern quarter of New Mexico Territory, Lincoln County was inadequately policed by one sheriff and a handful of deputies. A vast province of wide-open space and mountain hideouts, Lincoln was a haven for killers, rustlers, and outlaws of every stripe.

In 1873, for example, the notorious Horrell brothers, stock thieves and shootists, were chased out of Texas and arrived in Lincoln County with a herd of cattle late in the year. Shooting soon erupted in a cantina, and during the next few months thirty casualties were inflicted during the "Horrell War." Reduced in numbers, the Horrell boys fought their way back to Texas in January 1874. The Horrell War was a violent preview of the infamous Lincoln County War, which would involve John Chisum.

John Chisum and the term "Judge Lynch" soon became synonymous in Lincoln County. As Chisum continued to suffer large losses to stock thieves, he came to embrace the notion of summary justice. If Lincoln County was virtually lawless, its most prominent and powerful citizen soon would follow an extralegal tradition that extended into the American past for more than a century. Violence against British authority was commonplace in the colonies for several years prior to the American Revolution. The Boston Massacre (1770) and the Boston Tea Party (1773) were the most famous of scores of riots that began in the mid-1760s. In this atmosphere of unsanctioned violence, an outbreak of frontier crime in South Carolina triggered a response by angry citizens which launched the vigilante tradition in America. From 1767 through 1769, respectable citizens organized themselves as "Regulators" and tried troublemakers, flogging and expelling many undesirables. One outlaw gang was cornered, and sixteen members were slain.[3]

This successful Regulator movement inspired hundreds of similar actions during the remainder of the eighteenth century, throughout the nineteenth century, and into the twentieth century. While many Regulator groups were highly organized and operated on a comparatively large scale, others banded spontaneously to deal swiftly with a single criminal. These extralegal groups long were called "Regulators," but after the Civil War the customary term had become "vigilante."

Another term common to extralegal experiences was provided by Col. Charles Lynch, a prominent citizen of Bedford County, Virginia (the town of Lynchburg was named for Colonel Lynch). By 1780, with the Revolution still raging, Bedford County had became a hotbed of outlawry. Leading citizens formed a court with Colonel Lynch sitting as presiding judge. Regular—if illegal—trials were held, with flogging as the common punishment. This court thereby dispensed "Lynch Law," although in time this term came to mean a far more lethal form of justice than flogging.[4]

During the eighteenth, nineteenth, and twentieth centuries, more than 6,000 men and a few women were executed by vigilante activities. Vigilantism flourished on the frontier during the nineteenth century because the westward movement often outraced the establishment of courts, law officers, and even jails. Extralegal action was quicker and cheaper than any system of courts, judges, juries, attorneys, trials, appeals, and institutional punishment. Wherever lawlessness broke out, prominent citizens encouraged, organized, and usually led vigilante groups in establishing order.[5]

Certainly in frontier Lincoln County the westward movement extended beyond courts, law officers, and jails. Lincoln County was overrun by desperados and gunmen and rustlers, but the fledgling legal apparatus of the vast county could not yet cope with the lawlessness of this territorial frontier. "There was no law recognized," described one source, "no one could be found to fill the office of sheriff, and in no portion of the county was a man's life safe."[6]

The abandonment of the Bosque Redondo Reservation, where Navajos had tried to farm along the Pecos River, freed up range above Fort Sumner. Jinglebob cattle soon grazed as far north as Anton Chico and as far south as Carlsbad Springs, a distance along the Pecos of 200 miles. East of the Pecos, during rainy seasons when shallow lakes formed, Jinglebobs ranged far onto the Llano Estacado, causing roundup cowboys long rides. On the west side of the Pecos, Jinglebobs grazed sixty or more miles westward along the Penasco and Hondo Rivers.

John Chisum.
Courtesy Anderson–Freeman Museum,
Lincoln Historic Site.

But the enormous extent of Chisum's open range ranch exposed the cattle to stock thieves.[7]

Chisum submitted claims for losses to Indians totaling $143,995, even though he was not permitted to claim losses to warriors who were on the loose, unconfined to reservations.[8] After the Apache raids against his horse herds in the fall of 1874, confinement to the reservations steadily reduced Chisum's losses to war parties. Cattle rustlers, however, came to pose an even greater problem. He later explained to a reporter that "the thieving element which had come into the country seemed all at once to conceive the idea of engaging in the cattle business, and starting their herds from such cattle as they could steal from Mr. Chisum." Chisum's men branded 8,228 calves in 1874, but because of the sharp reduction of the horse herd, the cattle could not be properly handled for a time. As a result, in 1875 no more than 5,000 calves were branded and earmarked. Even in a normal year Chisum estimated that only three fourths of his calves were branded.[9]

Therefore there always were a great many unbranded and unmarked calves on Chisum's range. It was simple to apply a branding iron—perhaps a running iron—while on the range. If the calf had been through a roundup, the Long Rail brand could be altered, into an arrow for example. Little could be done about the Jinglebob earmark, which was on both ears, except for to cut off the dangling lower end of each ear. The "Jinglebob Ear" thus was converted to a "Lop Ear" mark.

Several hundred mutilated ears were found buried in a corral of Hugh Beckwith, whose little spread was north of the rustler haven of Seven Rivers. When Chisum heard of "suspicious activity" at Beckwith's place, he decided to investigate. Chisum had to ride to Arizona on business, but he sent Pitser—backed up by fast shooting foreman Jim Highsaw and several other armed riders—to check out the rumors. The discovery of the buried ears occurred in November 1876.

A few months later, on March 28, 1877, John Chisum and Jim Highsaw encountered Dick Smith. The subject of the Jinglebob ears came up, and "they plied questions which by nature implied his guilt." Soon Smith and Highsaw went to their guns, and Chisum's deadly foreman shot his adversary repeatedly.

"The killing of Dick Smith caused Uncle John some criticism," related Lily Klasner. Chisum was absent when a score of men from the Seven Rivers area rode up to South Spring in search of Highsaw. As this armed party approached the Chisum headquarters complex, Highsaw and his friends forted up in the Square House, a stout adobe which had been built for defense. With rifleman on top of the roof and gun barrels poking out of loopholes, the rustler gang shouted out a few curses, then rode away to the south. When legal action was initiated against Highsaw, he removed to Texas and continue to be known as a lethal gunman.[10]

When three mounts were stolen from a trail drive remuda, Chisum led a dozen riders in hard pursuit. One of the thieves was overtaken the next evening. "We asked him no questions," reported Chisum coldly. "Vegetation was scarce there but we took the highest we could find and dragged him up until his head was within two inches of the limb . . ." The rustler went through wild contortions as he strangled to death. "The buttons of his clothing gave way, and when we left him he was almost as naked as when he was born."[11]

Chisum described a similar incident to Lily Klasner. A cowboy shot a range foreman under "circumstances that made everybody condemn the killing." The cowboy witnesses appealed to Chisum for a ruling. "Now, we are away out here on the frontier where we have no regular court," he explained. "But we can proceed by law and organize the court of our own. We can probably make it just as fair as any regular court; we can hear evidence and be governed by our consequences. The law says a man shall be judged by his peers, and that means that you cowboys, who are the peers of the one that did the killing, are the ones to try him."[12]

Having heard Chisum's extralegal philosophy, the cowboys named a judge, a sheriff, a prosecuting "attorney," and twelve jury members. The cowboy was allowed to select a friend to defend him, the "court" was called into session, and a verdict of guilty soon was delivered. The cowboy asked Chisum to save him. "No, I have already said all I can and done all I can for you. These men would have hung you at once if I hadn't interfered and got them to give you a fair trial. I did so because I hoped something would come out of the trial to save you, but nothing of the kind has developed. These cowboys are your peers; they've been your companions and associates; they've given you a fair hearing; and this is their verdict. I don't see that I can do anything more for you. You won't be missed half as much as the man you killed will be by his widow and three children."

Having stated the key point in his last sentence, Chisum allowed summary justice to go forward. With no trees nearby, a wagon tongue was propped upright and a rope was threaded through the iron ring on the end of the tongue. The condemned cowboy was placed on horseback, a noose was fitted around the killer's neck, and "the horse was given a smart lick." Chisum finished his story to Lily Klasner that "it was a time-consuming matter to go to court," and since it was a matter of "cold-blood-ed murder, it was just as well to deal out justice and at the same time save the taxpayers money."

S.R. Coggin who, with his brother Moses, had a neighboring ranch to Chisum in Coleman County, Texas, came to Bosque Grande headquarters to buy a herd of steers from Chisum. Late in the day the wrangler, a popular youth, penned the *remuda*. But "a rough, surly" cowhand goaded the boy and called him a name. "I won't take that kind of talk," said the youngster.[13]

"You won't, eh?" growled the cowboy. "Well, you'll take this." He pulled his revolver and shot the young wrangler to death. Other members of the crew crowded around and asked what the trouble was. The quick triggered cowhand pointed at the dead youth and snapped, "The trouble's over now."

The young wrangler was a favorite with the cowboys, who seized the revolver and tied the killer's hands. Quickly they de-cided to string up the murderer as soon as they finished supper.

Coggin hurried to find Chisum. "John, you'll have to stop them, or they'll hang that man."

Chisum knew that his men shared his pragmatic notion of summary justice. "What can I do?"

"Send the man to Las Vegas," said Coggin, "let the law han-dle him."

"No, I'll stay out of it. It's fall branding time," explain Chi-sum, "and we are getting ready to gather up your steers. It would take a week to go to Las Vegas and back. Then, if the prisoner did not break out of jail, we would all have to stay for the trial. The men here are just as good judges and jury as you'll find in Las Vegas. I'll keep my hand out of it. He killed the boy.

Why not hang him?"

Judge Lynch had expressed the frontiersman's philosophy of extralegal justice. When the cowboys were finished eating, they mounted the condemned man on his horse. A rope was tossed over a cottonwood limb and a noose was fastened around the killer's neck. The horse was quirted out from under the doomed defendant, who was left swinging while the crowd dispersed. He was buried the next morning.

Judge Chisum remarked matter-of-factly to Coggin as the roundup crew rode out, "We are short two men, but we'll get along."

John Horton "Texas John" Slaughter bossed a member of trail drives before establishing his famous San Bernardino Ranch in southeastern Arizona Territory. On a stop at South Spring, Slaughter encountered a drunken Barney Gallagher, with whom he had experienced previous trouble. Gallagher rode toward Slaughter brandishing a sawed-off shotgun, but Texas John triggered a Winchester round that tore into Barney's leg and knocked him out of the saddle. The nearest doctor was at Fort Stanton, more than seventy miles away, and Gallagher bled to death several hours later.[14]

John Slaughter killed Barney Gallagher at the South Spring Ranch. Later he bought the San Bernardino Ranch in Arizona, and he and John Chisum enjoyed poker games together. *Courtesy Arizona Historical Society.*

Texas cowboy Gus Gildea helped deliver a cattle herd to South Spring a few days after John Slaughter killed Barney Gallagher,

whose "congealed blood" was still on the campground. Gildea was hired by Chisum, and it was not long until, "Two men
were tried by 'Judge Lynch' and executed . . ." Two shootings
took place, one at Bosque Grande and the other when a herd
was being brought to South Spring. "Both of these were for
cold-blooded murder," emphasized Gildea, "which was wit-
nessed by other cowboys who immediately arrested, tried,
convicted and executed the murderers, and went on with their
work as if nothing of so grim a nature had just happened. The
law of the range was 'forget it' for discussions were likely to
lead to trouble. In those days, cowboy law was enforced and
every cowboy knew it, and I never knew the subject again
brought up around the campfire."[15]

While riding a stagecoach out of Silver City, New Mexico, on
January 12, 1876, Chisum was one of the victims of a robbery.
Three highwayman stopped the stagecoach and ordered the
passengers to step outside. Chisum had $1,000 in cash, which
he slipped into his boot tops. He surrendered a small amount
of money from his pockets, while the robbers rode away with
$4,000 in silver bars being shipped to New York City.[16]

Later in the year, in October, Isaac Yopp was slain in a gun
fight at a Chisum cow camp on the Pecos below South Spring.
Yopp was in charge of the camp, and he suspiciously interro-
gated two of his cowboys, Buck Powell and Dick Smith, about
missing cattle. Yopp "became enraged" at Powell, pulling his
revolver and triggering three rounds. Powell unlimbered his
Winchester and shot Yopp in the mouth. Yopp dropped sense-
less to the ground. But within a moment he regained conscious-
ness and fired another shot. Powell desperately seized Yopp's
revolver and shot him in the heart.[17]

With violence and thievery a constant menace, Chisum
visited Fort Stanton. But the post commander would not send
out military details to protect private parties. Chisum next approached Lincoln County Sheriff William Brady, who also de-

Chisum was a visitor at the Commanding Officers' Quarters at Fort Stanton, ten miles west of Lincoln. Fort Stanton was headquarters for the Mescalero Indian agency, where Chisum sold beef herds. *Courtesy National Archives.*

clined to help because Seven Rivers, a rustler haunt, was in Dona Ana County. Without help from the authorities Chisum felt no qualms about meting out extralegal justice.[18]

In the fall of 1877 Apaches continued to slip away from the Mescalero Reservation and steal "a few" head of his livestock. Chisum led a large party of heavily armed men to the reservation. One version of the story stated that "Chisum succeeded in getting all the officers drunk," whereupon his riders "killed about 175" of the Mescaleros. Of course, if 175 reservation Indians had been massacred by white men, it would have become a notorious incident subject to severe historical scrutiny. It is equally unlikely that a civilian could have gotten an entire complement of officers inebriated. But if a few braves were caught off the reservation and slain, considering the attitudes of the time against Apaches, the famous story becomes more believable.[19]

Judge Chisum determined to make a show of force to rustlers at the southern part of Jinglebob range. He assembled thirty armed men from his cow camps in the Carlsbad and Seven Rivers area. On April 20, Chisum led his riders north along the river, past the adobe hamlet of Seven Rivers and on toward the ranch of Hugh Beckwith. At Beckwith's ranch they rounded up a number of horses and mules that were grazing, then rode more than a mile above Beckwith's residence to cut off water to the headquarters from an *acequia*. There were a few women and two Beckwith children at the ranch, but the next day a sniping duel took place at several hundred yards. No one was hit. While Winchester rifles could shoot that far, with open sights –which everyone probably was armed with—no one could hit a target beyond about 150 yards. On April 22 Chisum decided to break the stalemate by charging the adobe house. But his cowboys had no stomach for attacking fortified rifleman, "saying they were not going to get killed for $30 dollars a month, that they had hired to herd cattle and not to fight." Chisum lifted the siege, opened up the water supply, and even released the horses and mules he had appropriated.[20]

Chisum and his men returned to the roundup camp they had left a few days earlier. But Chisum fell ill and returned to his ranch. He went to bed, suffering from smallpox. A smallpox epidemic swept through eastern New Mexico, killing eighty citizens in Las Vegas. Chisum had never suffered a serious illness, but now he was bedridden and struggled through a long convalescence. His face was deeply pockmarked, although the pits eventually faded. Lily Casey Klasner reported that Chisum "treated the disfigurement jocularly and often said to the ladies and girls that though he had lost some of his good looks he still retained his winning ways."[21]

Chisum's illness and confinement kept him out of action long enough to end what has been called "The Chisum War" or "The Pecos War." So many men were killed along the Pecos —including a few whose bodies were dumped into the river— that a new verb entered the local lingo: "Pecoss'd."[22] Rustlers and other men had become embittered against Chisum, and he received death threats. Indeed, an even more violent conflict, the Lincoln County War would explode the next year, in 1878.

Chapter Six
Cow Country Finance

"We hear of cotton being king, of railroad kings, but J.S. Chisum of Bosque Grande is our stock king of New Mexico."

—Grant County Herald, Silver City

April 11, 1876.

B y the 1870s John Chisum had proven himself as a success-ful businessman of the Gilded Age. After the Civil War, a strong national demand for beef grew steadily, and Chisum met that demand on a larger scale than almost any other western rancher. Enterprising, opportunistic, visionary, optimistic, Chisum developed a business model that vaulted him to the pinnacle of a new and colorful industry. Other prominent ranchers—such as Richard King of the famous King Ranch; Charles Goodnight of the vast JA's; Walter Vail of Arizona's million-acre Empire Ranch; Alexander Swan who built the enormous Swan Land and Cattle Company; Dan and Tom Waggoner, father and son, who put together the immense Waggoner Ranch; Burke Burnett of the Four Sixes; C.C. Slaughter and his Long S and Lazy S ranches totaling more than 1.3 million acres—these men acquired title to great amounts of land and invested in capital improvements such as windmills, water tanks, stables, corrals, bunkhouses, residences. Corporate cattle companies established huge ranches with control of extensive ranges and large numbers of cattle and riders. Most ranches employed trail-driving outfits to deliver their cattle to distant markets, rather than take regular crew members away from their normal duties for extended periods of time.[1]

John Chisum remained resolutely committed to open range ranching on a large scale. The only property he purchased was for a headquarters complex, at Bolivar or Bosque Grande or South Spring. Occasionally a parcel fell into his hands, perhaps in payment for a debt. He declined even to lease rangelands, depending entirely upon free grazing for his enormous herds. Aside from headquarters buildings, Chisum built only cow camps at important points across Jinglebob range. He usually had a corral erected, along with a line shack of the most rudimentary construction—a dugout or small adobe. Otherwise, there were no capital outlays for land or improvements.

Chisum's hardy longhorns rustled successfully for themselves, in Texas and in New Mexico. Grazing was good in eastern New Mexico, and the Pecos and its tributaries provided adequate water. With no fencing on Jinglebob range, cattle could drift freely before winter storms. With such big herds, Jinglebob

Roping a steer on Chisum range in 1880s. JEH I.F 15.30.
Courtesy Haley Memorial Library.

A Chisum cowboy group, with a chuck wagon in background.
JEH I.F 15.17. Courtesy Haley Memorial Library.

cattle multiplied exponentially. Even as he filled large contracts, Chisum regularly maintained from 60,000 to 80,000 head of cattle on the vast reaches of the range he controlled.

Chisum bought cattle at every opportunity, beginning with his Denton County ranch. During 1867, with cattle thievery rampant on the Texas frontier and with the likelihood of beef contracts in New Mexico, "Mr. Chisum purchased off his neighbors many cattle, they being anxious to sell at any figure and on any terms . . ." Of course, Chisum's herds were made up of "large numbers of brands, which gave rise to many unpleasant stories affecting his honesty . . ." Anticipating problems because of his countless purchases, large and small, he kept a zinc tube with "a large roll of manuscripts, on which was recorded over 700 different marks and brands, and the number of cattle and each one he had handled, together with a power of attorney for each, a record so methodical and plain that it could not be questioned." Chisum often paid cash on the spot, or he signed notes, always with the cattleman's traditional handshake.[2]

Chisum shook hands and promised future payment on an especially large purchase from Robert K. Wylie. Wylie ranched near Chisum's Coleman County spread, and in 1872 he followed Chisum into New Mexico Territory. But the winter of 1872-73 was severe, and after a fierce snowstorm early in '73, Wylie stepped out of his dugout and could not see a single cow, not even with his telescope. Wylie had placed his herd on the range above Bosque Grande, but the norther had driven all of his animals to the south, where they mingled with Chisum's Jinglebobs. Wylie rode to Chisum's Bosque Grande headquarters and described the situation. Chisum had his customary good laugh at Wylie's quandary, then offered to buy Wylie's herd. The two friends arrived at a price of $60,000 for the scattered herd of 9,000 Wylie cattle. Chisum had contracts that he intended to fill after the spring roundup, and afterward, he

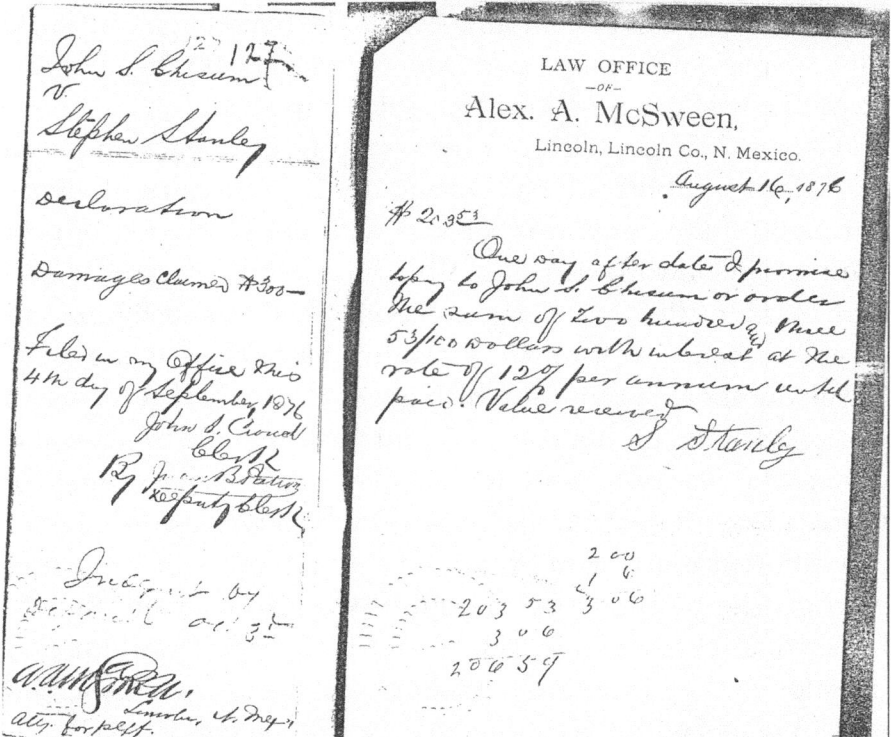

Attorney Alexander McSween handled numerous damage claims on behalf of John Chisum. Note Chisum's signature at upper left, as well as McSween's letterhead and his signature, at lower left. *Courtesy Southwest Collection, Texas Tech University.*

could pay Wylie. Until then the cattle would remain in Wylie's name while relieving Chisum of tax responsibility for the herd. Chisum and Wylie thus found themselves in a partnership arrangement. Wylie retained a ranching interest in Texas, but for the time being he stayed in New Mexico, establishing a cow camp on the east side of the Pecos about six miles above Carlsbad.[3]

A notable element of Chisum's huge ranching operation was maintaining an unusually large crew, numbering close to 100 men. With as many as 80,000 head of cattle on open range stretching almost 200 miles along the Pecos River, a great many riders were required to keep the cattle from scattering too widely. With nearly 100 men on the payroll, extra hands did not have to be hired for spring and fall roundups. And even though herd after the herd was sent to markets, cattle trailing contractors did not have to be employed. If several thousand cattle were to be delivered to fill a beef contract, Chisum divided the animals into two or even three manageable trail herds, which departed a couple of days apart. Chisum kept competent trail bosses on his crew, and sometimes Pitser led a trail herd. Chisum himself led trail herds, often for first-time delivery to new markets, such as Fort Bowie in Arizona Territory.

Fort Bowie was a major army post built during the 1860s in Apache Pass in southeastern Arizona. Chisum, an energetic seeker of beef markets, found a number of other markets in Arizona. In 1875 Chisum sent over 10,000 head of Jinglebobs to Arizona, in addition to 20,000 cattle his trail crews drove to Colorado, Kansas, and Missouri. As Chisum headed west into Arizona territory, the trial was clearly marked. From Jinglebob range a herd was driven west along the Hondo for nearly sixty miles. Angling southwest, the herd and crew passed through the White Mountains and skirted the southern White Sands. The trail led along the southeastern slope of the Oregon Mountains and through San Augustine Pass, opening onto a wide plain.

Fort Bowie in Arizona was a key outpost of the Apache Wars, and a frequent destination of Chisum and his cattle. *Courtesy National Archives.*

The herd forded the Rio Grande below Las Cruces, then headed west through Cook's Canyon and past Stein's Peek into Arizona. From August 1875 through January 1876 Chisum recorded monthly cattle deliveries to Fort Bowie, as well as larger herds monthly, from July 1875 through May 1876, to the San Carlos Reservation. These aggregate deliveries produced a gross income of $221,722 (Equivalent to $4.6 million today).[4]

Chisum often was on the range with his men, astride of a big roan called Old Steady and carrying binoculars.[5] He methodically penciled in names of the men he hired into a little black book. Employing such a large crew on a sparsely-settled frontier, Chisum had to take such men as made themselves available. Questions were seldom asked, and many of his riders were hard men who were good with a gun, such as James Highsmith. But Chisum was good at keeping morale strong with this crew. He hosted Christmas dances, as well as dinners and dances at Thanksgiving. Sometimes on roundups or trail drives, he unrolled an old cowhide for a makeshift dance platform. It was customary at all-male dances around the campfire or in a bunkhouse for some of the cowboys to tie a bandana around an arm and dance as a female partner. Chisum, of course, produced his violin and happily provided music. A cowboy named Bill Hudson was a fiddler, and Chisum often had him play after dinners at the ranch house. For these evening performances Chisum handed his good violin to Hudson.[6] Jinglebob cowboys composed a ballad verse as they returned to the ranch from a trail drive:

> When I get home, I'll sleep a week,
> And all those vows I make I'll keep.
> I swear by rope and bridle rein,
> I'll never drive jinglebob cows again.[7]

Chisum was absent from his ranch house half of the time, sometimes on the range or on trail drives, but often on business trips to market sources as distant as Kansas City. He bought fashionable attire for business travel, including a $750 dollar watch and an "expensive broadcloth suit which had been purchased on one of his visits to New York . . ."[8] But when he was on the range, he dressed in cheap, nondescript clothes. One visitor to the ranch saw Chisum "dressed in a 25¢ straw hat, 35¢ hickory shirt, and $1.50 pair of overalls. He had on no underclothes and no socks and a pair of $1.25 brogan shoes. He took some pride in and telling me of the outfit's cost . . . this was just one of his peculiarities."[9]

Despite his casual work clothes and his affable manner and his love of merrymaking, Chisum could crack a whip with his cowboys. One evening on the range a night herder rode into camp well before his relief was due. Apparently alert to everything that was going on even when he was in his bedroll, Chisum roused and realized that a night rider was not on duty, that the cattle had a better opportunity to drift or even to stampede. With no discussion, Chisum promptly fired the cowboy.[10]

On one occasion at Bosque Grande, Chisum's men went on strike for higher wages. Chisum calmly remarked that "he would just as soon strike a little himself" and that he could use the rest, and he paid off the men. (Indeed, at the height of his operations Chism's payroll exceeded $3,000 per month.) "Now you've struck," he stated firmly, "don't expect me to feed you." The cook, Old Beaver, later proclaimed that he would not strike. But as the aggravated cowboys prepared to leave, they decided to burn a rail brand on Beaver. "Then he'll be Chisum's for all time." A straight line was burned on one side of his ribs, and someone even cut his ear in a partial Jinglebob. The cook angrily threatened to poison anyone who tried to eat another meal at his chuckwagon. "If you come to the wagon," he warned, "they'll plant you tonight."[11]

In 1875 Chisum ran for a seat in the New Mexico Territorial Legislature. His only other venture into politics was as county clerk of Lamar County when he was in his twenties. After winning an election on his second try, Chisum quickly became dissatisfied with his new office, neglecting his county clerk duties and declining to run for reelection. In New Mexico, he must have thought that, despite the press of travel and the business of running an enormous ranch, he could benefit himself and his ranch from the Legislature. But he was not especially popular in New Mexico. There were rumors that Chisum had run roughshod over his few neighbors, stealing their land and livestock. Some of their cattle may have become mixed with Jinglebob herds, but he was not one to acquire the homestead titles of others. Of course, there were stories that he imposed range justice on men, and that he ran away from debts in Texas. For whatever reasons, Chisum only attracted ninety-three votes out of 433 cast.[12]

A significant question of debt followed him from Texas in New Mexico. In the spring of 1867, while Chisum still made his home at the Great White House near Bolivar, he was visited by a man named Wilber. Wilber explained he had a partner named Clark, that they were going into the beef packing business at

Fort Smith, Arkansas, and that "they wished me to go in with them as an equal partner in the business as I was a stockman." Wilber said that "we could pack from 10,000 to 15,000 beeves in the season and that the profit would be immense . . ." Chisum dubiously asked how much money Wilber and Clark could raise, and he was told $25,000. "That amount I informed him would not buy the salt and barrels we should need, and I added that if he went into such a business with such a small amount of money, his firm would prove a curse rather than a blessing both to them and to the stockmen."[13]

Chisum finally agreed that if the two partners would raise $66,666.67 "and invest it in a packing house, salt, and barrels," he would provide $33,333.33 in beef at market price. Wilber agreed to see Clark, and if they could raise the money Chisum required, they would write him and meet to draw up the agreement. Chisum was asked to write out and sign preliminary conditions, and the cattleman agreed, also writing out a copy for himself. Chisum said that he intended to make inquiries about Clark and after Wilber left the rancher wrote a friend in Arkansas. "The answer was, Clark, has got nothing and leave him alone."[14]

Chisum remained at his Denton County home for three months, never receiving a line from Wilber or Clark. "I have never seen Wilber since," wrote Chisum, "and I never did see Mr. Clark in my life." Chisum concluded, "that all idea of the packing business was abandoned . . ." In June 1867 he went to his range near the Concho River, and the next month he led his first herd to New Mexico. Chisum wintered the cattle around Bosque Grande, then left for Texas on April 5, 1868, arriving in Coleman County on May 8, 1868. At that point he learned that Wilber and Clark had begun packing beef at Fort Smith in the fall of 1867, operating the packing plant and a mercantile store under the label: "Wilber, Chisum & Clark."[15]

One of Chisum's brothers heard about the spurious firm

and traveled to Fort Smith to confront the "partners" of John Chisum. "Myself and Clark have taken the liberty of using your brother John's name," pleaded Wilber, "but don't say anything about it."

He exposed Wilber and Clark anyway, and their business-es closed the next day, although the firm was in debt $80,000 or $90,000. John Chisum heard all of this when he returned to Coleman County on May 8, and two days later he set out for Austin. He recorded that he consulted with Governor Elisha Pease, explaining the contract with Wilber and showing him the signed agreement. Governor Pease, who also was an attor-ney, advised Chisum to publish an announcement that he was not a partner of Wilber and Clark. Since he had not been in Arkansas during the life of the "partnership," Chisum's claim should be upheld. Chisum published his disclaimer in one Ar-kansas newspaper and two Texas papers. Although some Texas cattlemen brought suit, "The courts decided I was no partner of said pretended firm and was not responsible for contracts made by them." But the story followed him to New Mexico, where opportunistic men would provide the "curse" Chisum had predicted.[16]

Chisum might have benefited financially if indeed he had pursued the packing plant business. Texas ranchers sent mil-lions of cattle to market, but fortunes were made by out-of-state middlemen who operated stockyards or packing plants or com-mission firms. But Chisum did not want to organize and main-tain a packing plant. Or a major stockyard. Or a commission firm. With his knowledge of cattle and ranchers, Chisum could have achieved sustained success at any of these businesses. But he did not want to run a packing plant or a big stockyard. Noth-ing in a packing plant called out to him. The open range of the frontier West called to him, and so did wild longhorn cattle and wild—or at least half-wild—cowboys. The pioneer cattleman's way of life invigorated him. He led drives into his fifties. Chisum rode horseback—or mule back—into middle-age, and he camped out on drives and at roundups. He made long trips in search of markets. Chisum's lifestyle was physically demanding, but he responded with the stamina and vigor of a much younger man, and he relished his prominence in a challenging and colorful business. "We hear of cotton being king, of railroad kings," wrote an impressed reporter, "but J.S. Chisum of Bosque Grande is our stock king of New Mexico."[17]

"Chisum kept a close eye on all his ranch undertakings," related cowboy Frank Collinson. "He nearly always went with the boys to direct the work on the range . . ." Chisum's crew often kept cattle at horseshoe bends of the twisted Pecos River, with the outlets no more than 100 yards wide. "Since the Pecos has steep banks and innumerable bends, the river was handy on a roundup," Said Collinson. "At night the cowboys would put the herd into one of the bends and guard the outlet."[18]

Collinson stated that often 300 to 400 calves were branded from noon until evening. "Most of the Chisum cattle were wild and were handled by men just about as wild as the cattle. Always during roundup time, several cattle were killed by fighting bulls. Many horses were also hooked. When two bulls fought, one eventually turned around and always hooked a horse in its path. Occasionally a man was gored."[19]

During one of Chisum's large cattle drives, he learned that the herd following his was having a problem with recurring stampedes. Accompanied by one rider, A.B. Robertson, Chisum went back to the following herd. According to Robertson, within twenty minutes the cattle king spotted the troublemaker, "a steer with extremely wide and crooked horns, with one eye, and narrow between the eyes. Mr. Chisum ordered that the steer be cut out, driven down the river and killed . . . there were no more stampedes on that trip."[20]

Chisum's great success as a cattle king, as well as his legendary hospitality at his ranch, did not go unnoticed in New

Mexico Territory. A reporter from Las Vegas visited Chisum's ranch in 1875 and wrote a thorough description that his newspaper knew would interest readers:

> The Chisum ranch is situated on the Pecos River, New Mexico. It extends south along the river near Fort Sumner to Seven Rivers, a distance of 150 miles. This is the extent of the ranch north and south. East and West it reaches as far as a man can travel on a good horse during a summer, practically as far as stock can range from the river without water. The country on both sides of the river is high rolling prairie, covered with a thick, heavy growth of black grass, the most nutritious of grasses. The grass is knee-high on every hill and mesa this year. The river is the second in size in the territory and is fed from the snows in springs of the western mountains. To the eastward extends the Staked Plains from which side there is not a single tributary to the Pecos. The home ranch is at Bosque Grande, fifty miles below Fort Sumner. At this point the general store is kept, buildings and large corrals constructed. At convenient points up and down the river from the home ranch are secondary stations, or cow camps, which the herds occupy as temporary homes. Not less than 100 employees take care of the cattle. The expenses of Mr. Chisum, for horses the last ten years have been very heavy, due to losses from Indian raids. At one time, after an Indian foray, only ten head of horses were left on the ranch. The savages captured at that time three or four hundred head. The men had to herd on foot until other stock could be purchased. The horses have been of valuable quality, ranging from a dozen to 1000 head. This year, however, has been unusually quiet. The Indians have not committed a single depredation. The spring roundup will take place in February.[21]

This account did not mention Chisum's persistent problems over the Arkansas beef packing plant. Nor did it mention accusations over other unpaid debts. And nothing was said about cattle rustlers. During this period a rustler named Lucero was caught stealing Jinglebob cattle. Chisum was not present, and there was no extralegal hanging. But his men flogged Lucero and threatened to kill him if

COL. ROBERT D. HUNTER.

R.D. Hunter, who arranged the purchase of 60,000 head of Jinglebob cattle. *From Cox, Cattle Industry and Cattlemen of Texas.*

he committed stock theft again on Chisum's range. Stock theft became more regular than usual in the Seven Rivers vicinity, and at the slaughter pens at Fort Stanton, cattle began to be noticed with Jinglebob brands that had been altered: the "arrow" brand, of course, as well as the "pitchfork," the "lazy P attached to a rail," and the "pig pen." Chisum emitted his usual chuckle, but the laugh carried scant humor. "When they get to using my rail to build a pig pen, it is time for me to squeal."[23]

Since he owned none of the land he grazed, Chisum's cattle provided his only substantial asset. And with an estimated 80,000 head, natural increase soon replaced the cattle he sold to fill beef contracts. When a newspaper reporter found Chisum "in a deep reverie," in a "deep study," he asked the cattle king why he seemed uncharacteristically preoccupied. Chisum admitted, "I'm in trouble because I cannot dispose of my stock as fast as it increases."[24]

Furthermore, the range he needed to support his immense cattle herd was shrinking, as settlers moved in with homestead grants that took up small parcels of Jinglebob lands. In order to deal with large debts on cattle he had bought in Texas, Chisum took out a sizeable loan from Hunter, Evans & Company, a new livestock commission firm founded by R. D. Hunter and Albert G. Evans in 1873. Hunter immigrated as a child with his family from Scotland. As a young man, he became a successful cattle raiser and trader before establishing a major commission company with Albert Evans. Hunter, Evans & Company rapidly became one of the leading commission firms in the nation. Hunter, Evans & Company had "heavy Indian contracts," and livestock was the only way they could receive payment for their loan to Chisum.

"The ranch of John S. Chisum, of Bosque Grande, New Mexico was sold to Col. R.D. Hunter of St. Louis, the other day for $219,000, one-half cash down." This announcement was made by the Pueblo *Colorado Chieftan* on December 3, 1875. Another source stated that the sale price was $319,940. The

CAPT. ALBERT G. EVANS

Albert G. Evans, of Hunter & Evans, which dealt with John Chisum on a predictably vast scale. *From Cox, Cattle Industry and Cattlemen of Texas.*

negotiation was concluded in November 1875. Chisum was to deliver 60,000 head of cattle to Hunter, Evans & Company, and the firm would place most of the livestock on their extensive lands in Kansas, although some herds would be trailed directly to specific markets. Indeed, Chisum was asked to send as soon as possible 12,000 head of Jinglebobs to Arizona's San Carlos Agency. Hunter, Evans & Company immediately sent "221 fine bulls from Kentucky" to the Pecos Valley Range.[25]

A story circulated that R.D. Hunter rambled through Texas, buying up old notes signed by John Chisum for cattle purchases. According to the story, late in 1875 Chisum and Hunter arrived in Las Vegas to complete their massive transaction in the office of Thomas B. Catron, U.S. Attorney for the District of New Mexico. After final negotiations were agreed upon, Hunter supposedly pulled a satchel from Catron's safe. The satchel was stuffed with promissory notes Hunter had bought up for as little as ten cents on the dollar. Chisum then was paid off with his own notes and what was called Hunter's "legal rustle."[26] This story was widely told—gleefully told, in some quarters. But Hunter's reputation as a businessman would have been seriously damaged in the cattleman's world by such a shenanigan in a major deal, and Chisum also would have responded

HUNTER, EVANS & CO.,
COMMISSION MERCHANTS FOR THE SALE OF

LIVE STOCK

AT
NATIONAL YARDS, East St. Louis, Ills.,
AND
KANSAS STOCK YARDS, Kansas City, Mo,

Cash advanced on consignments to either House. Special attention given to the sale of Texan and Colorado Cattle.

Hunter, Evans & Co. business logo.
Courtesy Southwest Collection, Texas Tech University.

in some manner. Although it was a good story, there always are good stories about men of Chisum's prominence.

Hunter's firm and Chisum agreed that the rounding up and delivery of 60,000 cattle from an enormous range would take a couple of years or more. Chisum would be in overall control of the operation, salaried at $5,000 by Hunter & Evans as "superintendent" with "power of attorney to do business in New Mexico." But R.D. Hunter's younger brother, David, came to New Mexico with his family to represent the firm. It was arranged that Pitser Chisum, who had provided key services to his older brother for nine years, would receive $27,000 worth of cattle, which would be branded "U" on the left shoulder since the firm purchased the Long Rail brand. "Having the pick of the herd, and with a thorough knowledge of what constituted a first-class animal, [Pitser] was very careful to take only the best . . ."[26]

John Chisum knew that a substantial number of cattle would remain after final deliveries were made to Hunter, Evans & Company. But the Pecos range was being steadily reduced, and cattle theft continued unabated. Chisum no longer wanted to build a vast herd—he desired nothing more than a smaller herd of improved quality over his lanky, wild Texas longhorns. With cash available, he began to form ambitious plans for his South Spring location. For the next few years, Chisum would be busy with range activities, rounding up cattle, branding calves, hiring cowboys—and battling rustlers. The rustling problems proved to be part of a greater difficulty—a difficulty that would explode into the murderous Lincoln County War.

Chapter Seven
Chisum and the Lincoln County War

*"You might as well try to stop the waves of the
ocean with a fork as to try to oppose me."*

—L. G. Murphy

Lawrence G. Murphy was a major instigator of the notorious Lincoln County War, one of the most violent conflicts in the turbulent history of the Old West. The Lincoln County War exploded in 1878 with a wild succession of murders, shootouts, ambushes, and the five-day Battle of Lincoln. During the Lincoln County War a previously unimpressive young cowboy known as Billy the Kid emerged as a major western gunman and outlaw. The Kid's death at the hands of Sheriff Pat Garrett in 1881 marked the end of the Lincoln County War, and vaulted Billy to legendary status.

All of this homicidal action was triggered by the ruthless acquisitiveness of

L.G. Murphy, who ruthlessly attempted to dominate the economy of Lincoln County. *Courtesy Anderson–Freeman Museum, Lincoln Historic Site.*

Murphy erected "The House" the largest building in Lincoln.
Courtesy Anderson–Freeman Museum, Lincoln Historic Site.

Lawrence G. Murphy. Murphy was a teenaged Irish immigrant who enlisted in the army not long after arriving in America. He served two five-year enlistments and reached the position of regimental quartermaster sergeant of the Fifth Infantry. Murphy was discharged in 1861, shortly after the Civil War erupted, and he joined the First New Mexico Volunteers. Now a commissioned officer, he served throughout the war and attained the rank of major. Mustered out of Fort Stanton, the ambitious Major Murphy used his contacts to obtain lucrative government contracts to provide beef and other provisions for the nearby Mescalero Reservation. He organized the mercantile firm of L.G. Murphy & Co. and acquired a partner, Emil Fritz, who was an army associate in command at Fort Stanton. In 1869 the partners relocated to nearby Lincoln, and in 1874 Murphy erected the largest building in the little town to accommodate their business. L.G. Murphy & Co. moved into a big, two-story adobe which everyone called "The House." The House physically dominated the west end of Lincoln's only street. Murphy operated a store and a saloon downstairs, while living quarters

View of Lincoln looking eastward, with The House clearly visible, along with the town's single winding street. *Authors collection.*

and a Masonic Lodge Hall were upstairs.[1]

Murphy engaged with the "Santa Fe Ring," a corrupt polit-ical clique that operated from the Territorial Capital. He con-trolled the sheriff of Lincoln County, William Brady, another old army comrade. When Emil Fritz fell ill and returned to his father's home in Germany, Murphy elevated a young but ruth-less employee, James J. Dolan. Murphy also began ranching, steadily building a herd with cattle stolen from John Chisum's far-flung range. Land that Murphy did not own was sold to un-suspecting new settlers. Murphy used the monopoly enjoyed by his company to dominate the area economy.

New Mexico historian Warren A. Beck described Murphy at this time:

> An aggressive man, he soon controlled all business en-terprises in the area, so that few men were able to obtain work, prove title to their land, or even remain in the terri-tory if he disapproved. As he had the financial means and owned the only store around, the farmers and ranchers

were forced to buy from him at exorbitant prices in order to obtain credit. Since he also controlled most of the wagon trains, he was able to force the farmers and ranchers to sell their goods to him. By such means he was able to dominate the economic life of the surrounding countryside to such an extent that he was accused of being a virtual dictator.[2]

There was considerable resentment over Murphy's domineering control of the economy, but he hired a number of gunmen as enforcers. In addition to Sheriff Brady, his former comrade-at-arms, Murphy also enjoyed the backing of the Lincoln County District Attorney, William Rynerson, and United States District Attorney, Thomas B. Catron. "Even the territorial governor, [Samuel B.] Axtell," stated Beck, "had borrowed money from him and hence was in his debt."[3]

Murphy's ranching enterprise was comparatively small, but he regularly filled large beef contracts to the military and to Indian agencies. John Chisum realized that Murphy's men constantly were raiding his cattle. The "wholesale robbery of his herds" would affect the rounding up of the cattle for the transfer of Jinglebobs to Hunter, Evans & Company. Chisum began to push back, to the extent that "Mr. Chisum has by many been held responsible for . . . the celebrated trouble known as the 'Lin-

James J. Dolan, aggressive partner of L.G. Murphy. *Courtesy Anderson–Freeman Museum, Lincoln Historic Site.*

coln County War' . . ."[4]

Chisum found key allies in two young men of ambition and education who moved to Lincoln at the time of "the celebrated trouble." Alexander McSween was an attorney and a devout Presbyterian who came to Lincoln in 1875 with his wife Sue, a lovely and cultivated woman. An excellent attorney, McSween handled the legal affairs of The House, but became increasingly troubled by L.G. Murphy's questionable practices. Murphy's first partner, Emil Fritz, died of heart and kidney disease in 1874 in Germany. Fritz, who never married, left a $10,000 insurance policy, and Murphy claimed payment for a debt. McSween traveled to New York and pressed the claim successfully, but kept the large payment to cover his expenses. Murphy sued for embezzlement, but McSween was exonerated during the 1878 spring term of the Lincoln County District Court. John Chisum was present during the proceedings to lend support as a friend.

By this time McSween was in direct competition with The House. He had become friends and business partners with Englishman John Tunstall, who arrived in Lincoln County with family money to invest. Tunstall stayed at South Spring Ranch while Chisum advised him about locating a spread and assembling a crew. Tunstall soon established a ranch thirty miles south of Lincoln, and he and McSween

Alexander McSween, Lincoln lawyer who chose to stop representing the unscrupulous L.G. Murphy. McSween allied with Englishman John Tunstall and cattle king John Chisum. *Courtesy Anderson–Freeman Museum, Lincoln Historic Site.*

The Tunstall Store attracted many customers, and soon housed the Lincoln County Bank, with John S. Chisum as president. *Courtesy Anderson–Freeman Museum, Lincoln Historic Site.*

The interior of the Tunstall Store is maintained by the Lincoln Historic Site, and includes original display cases. *Photo by the author.*

opened a store to compete with The House. The new mercantile was down the street from The House, and quickly began to draw customers away from L. G. Murphy's monopolistic enterprise.

John Chisum became part of this opposition firm. He had engaged in mercantile enterprises since his youth, and he strengthened the firm by adding a banking operation, with himself listed as bank president. L.G. Murphy was furious at his competitors. Rustlers began to strike Tunstall's livestock, as well as Chisum's. Chisum received death threats. On August 18, 1877, the *Mesilla Independent* described recent activities of "small parties" of rustlers in the Seven Rivers area: "These men are threatening to kill Chisum wherever they can find him."

Murphy and Dolan utilized area newspapers, engaging in a letter-writing campaign against their competitors. A letter to the *Santa Fe New Mexican* later appeared, on June 7, 1878, in the *Arizona Miner* of Prescott:

> Lincoln County, New Mexico, seems to be undergoing a reign of terror. A lawyer by the name of McSween is largely responsible, according to reports from Murphy and Dolan. They also accuse J.S. Chisum, the cattle king, of being in with McSween and other parties making to defraud Murphy and Dolan, in New Mexico and Arizona.

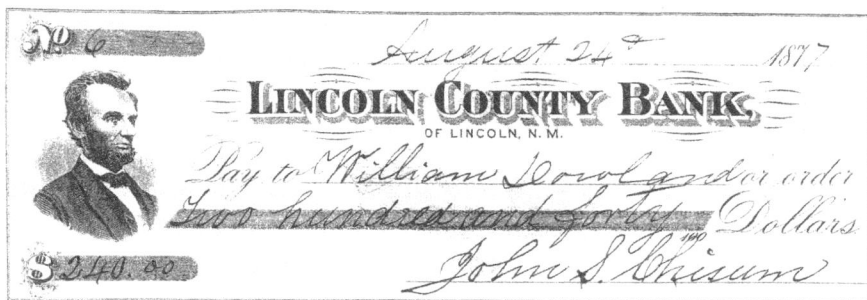

Chisum signed this check on his Lincoln County Bank.
Courtesy Southwest Collection, Texas Tech University.

On June 8, 1878, *The Great County Herald* published a letter by a partisan settler:

> I know that Chisum would be glad to see me killed and so I just left my crops and sailed out. Lots of men are leaving the country in the same way, because they say that McSween and… Chisum are paying four dollars a day for a man and his rifle and intend to drive everybody out.

After hostilities began the *Mesilla News* published the following notification on July 14, 1878. "John S. Chisum, it is reported, furnishes . . . McSween's boys with fresh horses to ride after they run from the sheriff—Chisum's house is also open to them to use as a fort against the officers of the law."

Indeed, the Square House at South Spring had been built to withstand Apache attacks. Large planks were placed horizontally into the thick adobe walls, so that warriors could not dig through. The walls were loopholed, and rifleman could be positioned on the flat roof, protected by an upper extension that lipped around the top of the entire building. On one occasion Alexander McSween and a few allies, including Billy the Kid, rode into the South Spring Ranch, trailed by a posse led by Deputy Sheriff Marion Turner. John Chisum was not present, but his brother James and Billy the Kid scrambled up to the roof. The posse pulled up at the corral and soon rode away. A few days later, however, some of the posse members returned. James Chisum approached them on foot to warn them that women and children were present and that they should not open fire. Heeding Chisum's advice, the posseman left the South Spring headquarters.[5]

One night during this tense period John Chisum met with several of his veteran riders inside the ranch house. McSween also was there, and so was Billy the Kid. Chisum warned his men that soon they probably would have to use their guns, and he assured them that they were free to leave with no hard feelings. J.K. Millwee, who had cowboyed for Chisum for six years, did not carry a gun and asked for his pay. Two other cowboys also left. Millwee returned to Texas and eventually owned his own ranch, but he never forgot the dramatic meeting in the Square House.[6]

Great animosity was generated against Chisum by Murphy and Dolan. In August 1877 Chisum visited Lincoln, accompanied by foreman George Hogg, and he stayed overnight in the McSween home. Late that night two gun happy drunks, Charlie Bowdre and Frank Freeman, staggered up and down Lincoln's winding street, firing their sixguns. Stopping at the McSween residence, they shouted that if "John S. Chisum or his corpse was not turned over to them, they would burn the d__d house down." They began shooting into the house, where there were women and children, but a return shot sent them stumbling away.[7] Within a few days Freeman was killed and Bowdre suffered the same fate in 1880 while riding with Billy the Kid.

Major Murphy became more closely involved with the Santa Fe Ring and became president of the First National Bank of Santa Fe. Perhaps because of inroads made in his Lincoln County operations by McSween, Tunstall, and Chisum, in April 1877 Murphy sold his mercantile interests to James J. Dolan and John H. Riley. But the senior partner of the renamed " Jas. J. Dolan & Co." was a violent man who twice had shot adversaries in confrontations in Lincoln. Dolan and Riley became increasingly concerned over the mounting financial difficulties of The House. Riley feared that Dolan would further damage their firm by reacting to their competitors in typical hair-trigger fashion.

Riley, a former soldier who was respected as a fighting man, confided his worries to rancher George Coe. "George, I am going to get out of this business. It's going to the wall. Do you know what it will mean if Dolan takes charge? He's a fighter, not a businessman. We're financially embarrassed now and there's plenty of grief ahead for somebody. "[8]

Perhaps hoping to escape some of the "grief" Riley feared, Alexander and Sue McSween and John Chisum decided to leave the trouble of Lincoln County for a holiday trip to St. Louis. The McSweens and Chisum planned to meet in Anton Chico, and Alexander and Sue departed Lincoln on December 18. From Anton Chico, the trio of travelers moved on to Las Vegas, intending to journey toward Trinidad, Colorado, where they would board a train for St. Louis.

But in Las Vegas they encountered the sheriff of San Miguel County, who presented warrants from U. S. District Attorney Thomas B. Catron and from Lincoln County District Attorney William L. Rynerson. Chisum was roughed up by a make-shift posse and jailed under charges of resisting arrest, while McSween was permitted to post bond.

McSween was escorted back to Lincoln to address the charges against him, but Chisum languished in custody in Las Vegas for several weeks. He hired a lawyer, and while the legal wheels turned he wrote a vindication: "HOW I WAS IMPRIS-ONED *AND FOR WHAT*." It was dated "Las Vegas, January 16th 1878," and Chisum's stated purpose "is to place myself properly before the business world." In a letter to Ash Upson of Roswell, Chisum expressed his customary aplomb: "It is natural for us all to think at times that we are badly treated and sometimes I think I am treated a little wrong but I reckon not." A week later he was in high spirits: "I have a cat that is faithful. It never leaves my room and it's full of fun and I have a fiddle and I am well fed . . ." A few days later Chisum gleefully reported to Ash Upson that: "The sheriff took a fright last night" after hearing a rumor "that a big lot of my friends were going to take me out of jail . . ."[9]

Chisum soon was released and returned to his South Spring Ranch. Tensions were steadily worsening, and one of the gun-men Chisum hired during this tumultuous period was Henry

Brown, who until recently had worked for L.G. Murphy and The House. At the age of nineteen, in 1876 in the Texas Panhandle, Brown shot a fellow cowboy to death during an altercation in a cow camp. Gravitating to lawless Lincoln County, Brown signed on as a cowboy—and rustler—at Major Murphy's Carisosa Ranch.

By late 1877 Brown was able to state: "I have often heard the 'House' say they would have Alex. A. McSween killed." In December 1877 John Tunstall,

The deadly gunman Henry Brown offered his services, at different times, to both sides of the Lincoln County War, and at one point he was in the employ of John Chisum. *Courtesy Kansas State Historical Society, Topeka.*

in his capacity as vice–president of the bank, refused to cash a Dolan & Co. check. Dolan was furious and in Brown's presence snarled "that when the time came, and he got ready, he would kill Tunstall." But Brown found it increasingly difficult to collect his wages. He left The House, grumbling that "they cheated me out of what was and is justly due to me; but as I could not help myself I had to take what they gave me."[10]

Resentfully pocketing his unsatisfactory earnings, a surly Brown determined to join Dolan's opponents. Outspoken and bitter about the nonpayment of his wages by The House, Brown quickly found employment with John Chisum. If Chisum had second thoughts about hiring someone suspected of rustling cows from his herd, certainly Brown was not the first questionable character to be employed by the cattle king. And Brown brought not only a good gun but fresh information from

The House and its leaders.

Brown soon was assigned to the Tunstall ranch, along with such other gunhands as Billy the Kid, who had killed his first man at seventeen. The level of threats and harassment against John Tunstall increased ominously. Dolan obtained a writ of attachment against Alexander McSween and John Tunstall over the Fritz insurance matter. Sheriff Brady, working as closely with Dolan as he had previously with L.G. Murphy, levied the attachment, on February 10, 1878, against McSween's house, furniture, and store. Brady then dispatched Deputy Sheriff J.B. Matthews, who was a Dolan & Co. employee, and a large posse to attach the property of Tunstall's ranch.

On February 13 the posse arrived, but Tunstall's foreman Dick Brewer persuaded Deputy Matthews to leave the attached livestock at the ranch for the time being. But while this discussion was going on, posse member Frank Baker was heard muttering to Andrew "Buckshot" Roberts about Tunstall: "What the hell's the use of talking? Pitch in, and fight and kill the son of a bitch."[11]

Five days later Tunstall, who was determined to avoid bloodshed, headed for Lincoln with sev-

Bob Olinger rode for Chisum before pinning on a deputy's badge in Lincoln. He was killed during Billy the Kid's jailbreak. *Courtesy Anderson–Freeman Museum, Lincoln Historic Site.*

eral horses. Tunstall was accompanied by foreman Brewer and cowboys Billy the Kid, John Middleton, and Joe Widenmann, along with Henry Brown and Fred Waite, who followed in a supply wagon. The half dozen cowboy-gunmen were present to protect Tunstall in case of danger. Although their concern proved justified, their service as bodyguards was a dismal failure.

About twenty miles south of Lincoln two dozen armed riders materialized and cantered toward Tunstall. Brewer and Widenmann had ridden ahead

John Henry Tunstall hoped to make a fortune in Lincoln County, but his murder triggered an explosion of violence. *Courtesy Anderson–Freeman Museum, Lincoln Historic Site.*

to hunt wild turkeys, while Brown and Waite were far back in the wagon. When the hostile riders appeared, the Kid and Middleton warned their boss, then galloped away. But Tunstall turned his thoroughbred mount toward the posse to challenge them for being on his ranch. Abruptly the Englishman was shot out of his saddle, probably by Billy Morton, and rustler Jesse Evans triggered a round into the fallen man's brain. Tunstall's thoroughbred also was killed.

Word of Tunstall's death spread like a prairie fire, and within hours armed men were riding into Lincoln to align themselves with the Dolan or McSween factions. By nightfall on February 18 at least sixty gunmen were gathered at McSween's store. John Chisum was there; Billy the Kid and Henry Brown rode up within several hours; and after dark Dick Brewer, wary that "the s_ _ _ _ _ b_ _ _ _ _ Murphys would kill him," arrived at the back door. Chisum and McSween were offering wages of five dollars a day for recruits.[12]

The next day a coroner's jury named Frank Baker, Billy Morton, Jesse Evans, George Hindman, Tom Hill, James Dolan and "others not identified" as the victim's assailants, and Justice of the Peace John B. Wilson issued warrants for the accused men. Lincoln Constable Antanacio Martinez deputized Billy the Kid and Fred Waite to assist him in serving the warrants, but before this trio could act they were jailed by Sheriff William Brady for disturbing the peace. Although their detention was brief, the Kid was furious. Three days after the homicide, Tunstall's body was brought into Lincoln, and a grim funeral service on February 22 triggered more oaths of vengeance. Tunstall was buried behind his store, and Sue McSween's small organ was carried from the McSween residence, next-door to the east, to enhance the outdoor service.[13]

Dick Brewer, Tunstall's foreman as well as owner of his own spread, provided the leadership which united these vengeance-seeking gunmen. Enraged at the murder of his likable employer, he wangled an appointment as a special deputy from the cooperative John Wilson. Armed with his commission and several arrest warrants,

Tunstall foreman Dick Brewer, who was killed after becoming leader of the Regulators. *Courtesy Anderson–Freeman Museum, Lincoln Historic Site.*

he began to assemble a group of Tunstall sympathizers who achieved notoriety as the "Regulators." Brewer's original posse consisted of Billy the Kid, Charlie Bowdre, Henry Brown, Fred Waite, William McCloskey, Frank McNabb, John Middleton, J.G. Scurlock, and Sam Smith. These "constables" learned that some of the men they sought were on the Pecos River near Chisum's South Spring Ranch.

On March 6 the Regulators chased down Billy Morton and Frank Baker after a five-mile running fight. Morton and Baker surrendered their guns, but Brewer ominously voiced his regret that they had chosen to give up, another posse member had to be restrained from shooting the unarmed men, and there were threats about killing Morton and Baker on the trail. After a brief stop at Chisum's ranch, the posse and their prisoners headed towards Lincoln. About halfway between Roswell and Lincoln, Morton and Baker were shot to death, along with Regulator William McCloskey, who tried to stop the murders.

Sheriff Brady and other officials denounced the killings as murder, but the shadow of legality imposed by Wilson's official status saved the Regulators from indictment. Territorial Governor Samuel B. Axtell recently had come down to Fort Stanton to investigate the worsening feud and, af-

Billy the Kid, a gun-crazy rustler, killer, and fugitive. *Author's collection.*

ter a hearing in nearby Lincoln, he stripped Justice of the Peace Wilson and Brewer's posse of their authority. But the Regulators roamed the hills, restless for more action. On April 1, 1878, Billy the Kid and several other Regulators set an ambush in Lincoln from behind a plank fence adjacent to Tunstall's Store. As Sheriff Brady led four of his men down Lincoln's street, the Kid and other Regulators raised up and opened fire. Brady was dead when he hit the ground, while deputy George Hindman collapsed, mortally wounded and begging for water.

Three days later Dick Brewer led a fourteen-man posse into Blazer's Mill for a noon meal. They encountered Andrew L. "Buckshot" Roberts, a rugged old gunman who was trying to leave the country before the Regulators caught up with him. But shooting broke out, and Charlie Bowdre drilled Roberts through the mid-section. Roberts wounded George Coe and John Middleton, then shot Dick Brewer through the eye from long range before succumbing to his own wound.[14]

There were other encounters in the countryside, including a Fourth of July clash around Chisum's South Spring Ranch. According to George Coe, he and his cousin Frank Coe, Billy the Kid, and "two others" decided to spend the Fourth of July at a celebration hosted by John Chisum, who was not one to let a blood feud interfere with holiday festivities. During their sixty-mile ride the five cowboy/gunmen were trailed by enemy riders and

Sheriff William Brady, a Murphy–Dolan partisan, was ambushed and slain in Lincoln by Billy the Kid, Henry Brown, and three other Regulator gunmen. *Courtesy Anderson–Freeman Museum, Lincoln Historic Site.*

there was a long-range Winchester exchange between the two parties. On July 3 the Regulators arrived at South Spring and were welcomed by Chisum, who announced the next morning that a feast would be held that day. In high spirits, the Kid, George and Frank Coe, and two unidentified saddle pals rode six miles north to Ash Upson's store at Roswell. They procured tobacco for themselves and candy for Sallie Chisum, John's teenage niece.

The five Regulators left Upson's and headed back to the ranch about ten o'clock on the morning of July Fourth. But fifteen to twenty hostile riders soon appeared and a running fight continued during the quick retreat to Chisum's headquarters. George Coe, the Kid, and a few others positioned themselves on the roof of the Square House, and random sniping continued until nightfall. The Regulators took turns climbing to the roof and keeping their adversaries at bay. "They were out of gun range all day," reported George Coe. It was a unique way of celebrating the nation's 102nd birthday. By dawn the invaders had withdrawn, and Regulators in force rode out to follow their trail. When it was discovered that their assailants were headed toward Lincoln the chase was abandoned.[15]

With danger in the air, Alexander McSween left Lincoln and took refuge in the countryside during late June and early July. As many as a score of men rode with him as bodyguards, including Billy the Kid, Henry Brown, George and Frank Coe, and other former Regulators, along with Hispanics, who reflected a general dislike by the native population of the domineering Murphy and Dolan. McSween and his men provisioned their camping expedition at Chisum's South Spring store, and when trailed by a posse in July they rode to the Square House. The posse turned back, but McSween collected more than forty men and rode to Lincoln, arriving on the night of July 14 and setting up a climactic battle.

John Chisum already had removed himself from the center

of this volatile conflict. Prudently he traveled to Bosque Grande, to superintend the collection of cattle he had sold to Hunter & Evans. This work was a legitimate responsibility of Chisum's, but he only would hear second-hand accounts of the remaining events of the Lincoln County War. Chisum's chief rival, L.G. Murphy, also was absent from Lincoln. Seriously ill, Murphy stayed in Santa Fe, where he died of cancer on October 20, 1878, at the age of forty-seven.[16]

When McSween reached Lincoln on July 14, he and thirteen of his men quietly barricaded themselves inside his residence. While an almost equal number of opponents slumbered up the street at The House, the balance of McSween's supporters positioned themselves at structures from which they could protect the rambling residence. Several men were stationed inside the *torreon*, a stone tower east of McSween's which once had served as a defense against Apache war parties.

Early the next morning Regulators, led by the Kid, began firing upon their startled adversaries. But two days of sporadic sniping produced only two casualties, a horse and a mule. On the third day the Regulators severely wounded a deputy, and on the fourth day a large detail of troops arrived from Fort Stanton. The military camped in the east end of town and declared their intention of staying out of the fight. But a number of McSween men were intimidated. By the fifth day, July 19, more than half of the McSween force had slipped across the Rio Bonito, which ran behind the McSween house, and vanished into the rugged countryside, abandoning their allies inside the residence, as well as a few other stalwart Regulators positioned elsewhere.

McSween's adobe house was a twelve-room, U-shaped building with four rooms in front and four in each of the east and west wings. On the final day the rear portion of the west wing was set afire, and the blaze fed on rafters, flooring, and window framing. McSween and his gunmen, in an attempt to create a fire break, pulled up floor boards and moved furniture into the most distant rooms in the house, but still the fire spread. Sue McSween and two other women were evacuated under truce, exiting from the still flameless east wing.

When darkness fell, only the three rear rooms of McSween's east end remained standing. When a breakout was attempted the attackers were waiting. Volley upon volley of gunfire flashed through the darkness as the trapped gunmen tried to shoot their way to safety. McSween resolutely refused the weapon offered him and marched boldly toward his enemies— armed only with a Bible clutched to his chest. He was shot dead. Several other gunmen were slain or badly wounded, including nineteen-year-old Robert Beckwith, one of the attackers who may have been hit by friendly fire.

But Billy the Kid was one of those who managed to escape. And Henry Brown, George Coe, and another Regulator, who now were positioned in a nearby warehouse, used the diversion at McSween's to slip away into the darkness. From a hilltop across the river, escaped Regulators could see the victorious enemy drink, dance, and laugh by the flickering light of McSween's burning house. The Tunstall store next door was looted, and so was Chisum's bank. By the next night most of the Regulators had reunited at the village of San Patricio, comparing escape stories. They all were afoot, and they had to find horses and gear. Most of the former Regulators drifted apart, but the Kid and several others rode north ninety miles to Fort Sumner.

Fort Sumner was to become a hideout and a haven for the Kid, and he announced his friends: "I propose to stay right here in this country, steal myself a living, and plant everyone of that mob who murdered Tunstall if they don't get the drop on me first . . . I need *dinero*. I'm broke fellows, and I've got to make a killing."[17]

George Coe decided to return to Lincoln and tried to straight-

en out his life. But Henry Brown, Tom O'Folliard, Charlie Bowdre, Fred Waite, and John Middleton elected to steal horses with
the Kid. Soon the gang drove 150 stolen horses across the Pecos
River and into the Texas Panhandle, camping for a time beside
the Canadian River just below rowdy Tascosa.

John Chisum also departed New Mexico for the Texas Panhandle. Both of his Lincoln partners, John Tunstall and Alexander McSween, had been murdered. Death threats had been
made against John Chisum and his brothers, Pitser and James.
John Chisum had spent several weeks in confinement in Las
Vegas with scant legal justification. Even after the Battle of Lincoln there were frequent shootings throughout Lincoln County,
and livestock theft remained rampant. Chisum and his brothers
decided to move their remaining cattle to the Canadian River in the sparsely settled Texas Panhandle until conditions improved in New Mexico. While preparations were being made,
John Chisum drove in a buckboard to Las Vegas. Arriving in
mid-August, he attended to business matters for the next few
weeks.

Meanwhile, several thousand head of Chisum cattle, now
branded with a U on the left shoulder, were rounded up,
along with a remuda of 150 horses. Two baggage wagons were
packed. James Chisum readied his children, Sallie, Will, and
Walter, for an overland journey and an extended stay. Charlie
Neebow would be in charge of the trail drive. From Bosque
Grande the caravan headed up the east bank of the Pecos River,
uniting with John Chisum at Fort Sumner. After passing Fort
Bascom the caravan reached the southern drainage of the Canadian River.[18]

The Canadian is the largest tributary of the Arkansas River. It is 760 miles long, running west to east 190 miles across
the Texas Panhandle. The Chisum expedition crossed the Texas
border on September 28, 1878. About ten miles east of the New
Mexico line, Trujillo Creek empties into the Canadian River

from the south. Near the mouth of Trujillo Creek dugouts and corrals were built. The Chisum camp was about thirty miles west of Tascosa, an adobe village which was just a couple of years old. But Tascosa was the only town in the Texas Panhandle, aside from Mobeetie well to the north, and a Chisum supply wagon could be sent to Tascosa for provisions.[19]

Chisum did not return to South Spring from Texas until November 1879. He estimated that by then he had lost "over 10,000 head" of cattle to rustlers through the years.[20] Hunter & Evans had completed the gathering of their immense herd from Chisum range, and the Hunter family had departed. Territorial Governor Samuel Axtell was removed from office in September 1878 and, within the month, General Lew Wallace was appointed to the post. Governor Wallace announced an amnesty for men involved in the Lincoln County War, and rustler/gunman Billy the Kid surrendered, then recanted. The Kid continue to steal livestock and, as often as possible, to slip into Fort Sumner, where he had friends and sweethearts.

Supposedly the Kid confronted John Chisum at Fort Sumner in the spring of 1880. The story was passed down from James Chisum to his son Will. According to the story, the Kid insisted that Chisum owed him $500 for his services during the Lincoln County War. The Kid threatened Chisum with his revolver. "Billy," replied Chisum calmly, "you know as well as I do that I never hired you to fight in the Lincoln County War. I always pay my honest debt. I don't owe you anything . . ." Billy instead swore to take his wages through stolen cattle.[21]

If this confrontation actually occurred in the spring of 1880, the Kid recently had gunned down another victim. On January 10, 1880, Billy the Kid killed a gunman named Joe Grant in a Fort Sumner saloon. Later in the year John Chisum supported Pat Garrett in a successful campaign for sheriff, and the towering former buffalo hunter and cowboy launched a manhunt for Billy the Kid and his confederates. Only a few weeks after taking office, Sheriff Garrett sprang an ambush at Fort Sumner against the Kid and five gang members. Tom O'Folliard was fatally wounded, and four days later the other outlaws were cornered at a hideout. Charlie Bowdre was killed and the Kid and the others surrendered. The Kid was tried and sentenced to hang on May 13, 1881. Incarcerated in Lincoln at the two-story courthouse – the former Murphy-Dolan store—on April 26 the Kid killed two guards and escaped. One of the guards was beefy Bob Olinger, a former cowboy/gunman who once had ridden for John Chisum.

John Chisum apparently was instrumental in backing Pat Garrett for sheriff of Lincoln County, with the primary purpose of tracking down Billy the Kid. *Courtesy Anderson–Freeman Museum, Lincoln Historic Site.*

The Kid remained at large for two and a half months, tempting fate by remaining in the vicinity of Fort Sumner. Governor Wallace posted a $500 award for the capture of the Kid. On the night of July 14, 1881, Sheriff Garrett encountered Billy the Kid in a darkened room at Fort Sumner. Garrett killed the Kid with his first shot, helping to create a Wild West legend for his youthful victim. During the last four years of his life, from the age of seventeen through twenty-one, the gun crazy Kid fought in at least sixteen shootouts, ambushes, and running fights. Billy the Kid killed four men and helped to gun down four or five others. He was a western gunfighter of the first rank, but now he was dead. And with the death of its most legendary figure, the

Sheriff Garrett killed Billy the Kid in the front corner bedroom at this former officer's quarters at Fort Sumner. *Courtesy Anderson–Freeman Museum, Lincoln Historic Site.*

Lincoln County War was at an end.

As Lincoln County became more orderly, and with the homicidal Billy the Kid in a grave at Fort Sumner, John Chisum felt liberated to enjoy a splendid new ranch home at South Spring and to embrace a welcome change of lifestyle.

Chapter Eight

Simpaticas:
Housekeepers and Other Lady Friends

"John Chisum was one of the men whom
the Southwest should delight to honor."

—Lilly Casey Klasner

By the time John Chisum moved to New Mexico he was a confirmed bachelor. He was a natural flirt who enjoyed female company throughout his life. He was courtly and fun-loving, always ready to laugh and joke. When he had a lengthy courtship in his early twenties, he praised Sue Holman for being "ready for a joke at any and all times."[1] But Chisum was clerking for wages at the time, and felt that he could not yet support a wife. He delayed talk of marriage until Sue finally decided to wed another beau. By the time Chisum found an occupation that promised an outlet for his driving ambition, his twenties had passed without a wife. And in his thirties and forties and into his fifties Chisum focused his immense abilities on becoming one of the greatest ranchers in the nation.

Aside from Chisum's consuming drive for success there was another likely reason he never committed to marriage. His mother died when he was thirteen, an age at the beginning of puberty. Dorothy Bramblett was a brilliant teacher of psychology and a long time faculty colleague of mine at Panola College. I have asked her for assistance in analyzing other characters I have written about in the past, and I enlisted her to help me understand John Chisum. It was explained to me that thirteen or fourteen is perhaps the most difficult age for a boy to lose his mother. The loss of the most important female figure in his life when he is beginning puberty inflicts a hurt that often generates a lifelong fear of letting another woman become too close. Perhaps this subconscious fear helps us to understand why Chisum, despite his genuine affection for women, never took on the responsibility of a wife.[2]

Chisum also responded to the age-old family role of the eldest son. He was only fifteen when his older sister married and left the home. But he provided strong guidance and support for his three younger brothers. Jeff Chisum had health issues and he killed a man in Paris. John brought him to New Mexico, although Jeff soon died. Pitser Chisum became John's right-hand man in his ranching kingdom. And when James Chisum's wife died in Texas, John persuaded him to move with his three children—Sallie, Walter and Will—to the South Spring Ranch. Indeed, John's pretty niece, Sallie, became the hostess at his busy ranch home, and both her brothers became Chisum employees.

Sallie Chisum was preceded as hostess/housekeeper by John's first cousin, Frances Johnson Towery. The two cousins were close since childhood. In 1858 John bought a mulatto slave named Jensie from Frances and her husband Tom Towery. John was in need of a housekeeper at his Denton County ranch home, and Jensie brought three small children with her. There were rumors that Jensie became John's mistress, and that one or two of her children were fathered by John. All three of her children were born before coming to Chisum's ranch, and alternate rumors were widespread that some or all of Jensie's offspring were Towerys. Jensie worked for Chisum for five years, until 1863. It can never be known with certainty if John and Jensie were lovers. But when Chisum began moving his ranching operation to Coleman County, he installed Jensie and her children in a boarding house in Bonham. Chisum rarely returned to Paris after moving to West Texas and then to New Mexico, and it seems unlikely that he ever saw Jensie or her children again. Of course, Jensie and her children became free at the end of the Civil War in 1865.[3]

Another youngster who was bought as a slave by Chisum stayed with the cattle king until his death. Frank was born about 1855, and he was purchased by Chisum as early as 1861. Frank was somewhat crippled from birth, but he became a fine rider, and in time he was assigned as Chisum's horse wrangler. Deeply loyal to his boss, Frank adopted "Chisum" as his last name. Frank Chisum made the move to Coleman County, and after 1870 the teenage cowboy joined the crew in New Mexico. Frank saved his wages and in 1878 he purchased 200 yearlings. When the Chisums moved to the Texas Panhandle with their reduced herd, Frank Chisum brought his cattle too. Frank was a member of the household as an attendant to his boss, and he remained at Chisum's side when John suffered with smallpox in 1877. After Chisum's death, Frank moved into Roswell. He grew his herd and became a prosperous rancher. Frank Chisum married three times. He died in his seventies in Wichita Falls in 1929.[4]

Tom and Francis Towery had hoped to move to California as early as the late 1850s. John Chisum brought them part of the way in the 1870s, inviting them to visit his vast open range ranch in New Mexico. Cattle buyers, ranchers, cowboys, and passersby constantly dropped in at Chisum ranch headquarters, first at Bosque Grande and later at South Spring. Adding to the traffic were holiday meals and dances, which often went on for two days. Chisum needed the services of Cousin Frances as hostess and housekeeper. Her son worked as a cowboy for Chisum, while Tom opened a saddle and harness shop. The Towerys finally left for California late in 1877, settling in Visalia. A black woman named Mary Ann had come to New Mexico with Chisum, and her duties including household chores. Mary Ann took over as housekeeper when Frances Towery departed.

The arrival of pretty, personable Sallie Chisum at the end of 1877 would solve Chisum's hostess vacancy.[5]

In New Mexico Chisum met and charmed a bright and impressionable young lady named Lily Casey. He talked at length with her through the years, and she proved to be a keen listener who had the knack of drawing him out. Later in life, as Lily Casey Klasner, she wrote an analytical manuscript that eventually was published as *My Girlhood Among Outlaws*. Her recollections and reflections about Chisum offer depth about "Uncle John" that is unavailable elsewhere.

"He always liked to talk, and on such occasions he spoke freely on all sorts of matters about himself and his business," revealed Lily. "It was through these conversations that I, though but a girl in her teens, came to know more fully about his life and character than many an older person."[6]

Lily was the third of seven children of Robert and Ellen Casey. She was born in 1862 near Fort Mason on the Texas frontier. Robert Casey was a U.S. Army veteran who remained near his former duty station as a rancher. He knew John Chisum in Texas and would renew their friendship in New Mexico. In 1867 Casey moved his family and 1,800 head of cattle to a ranch and grist mill located on the Rio Hondo about twenty miles south of Lincoln. The journey from Texas was filled with hardships and Indian troubles, and life on the new ranch also was hard and dangerous. Although still a child, Lily was pressed into duty as a cowgirl, becoming an excellent rider and an expert with a rope. Robert Casey prospered as a rancher and miller, and after selling a cattle herd he opened a well-stocked store beside the road at his spread. The store proved popular with travelers and customers at the mill—and it competed with the Murphy–Dolan mercantile in Lincoln.

At this time Chisum's ranch was headquartered at Bosque Grande, about forty-five miles northeast of the Casey home. Chisum's business generally took him to Las Vegas or Fort Sumner, farther still. But in 1873 he acquired a farm adjoining the Casey Ranch, and when Chisum came to inspect his new property, Robert Casey rode over to bring his old friend to his home. "To the children the coming of this man was an epochal event," remembered Lily. As Robert Casey and his guest approached their house, store clerk Abneth McCabe, who had worked for Chisum, was asked if it was really John Chisum. "Yes, that's him," said McCabe. "I can tell his walk. Nobody else walks like him." As the two men came closer, McCabe pointed out certain identity. "Listen to that laugh, everybody. That's him, alright enough; nobody else laughs as easily or as heavily as he does."[7]

Chisum immediately won the children over "in his genial way." He was impressed with Robert Casey's improvements. And after he moved his ranch headquarters to South Spring in Lincoln County, Chisum traveled often into the county seat in Lincoln, and "he invariably stopped at our place."[8]

Tragedy struck the Casey family in 1875 when Robert was murdered in Lincoln by William Wilson, a gunman hired by Murphy and Dolan. Murphy's role was not yet known when he presided at the burial services at the Casey home. Casey was well-liked and Wilson was almost lynched. Instead there was a trial and Wilson became the first man to be legally hanged in Lincoln County. But when he was cut down and placed in a coffin it was discovered that Wilson was still breathing. Casey's friends angrily pulled him out of the coffin and strung him up again.

Not surprisingly, rustlers began to steal both horses and cattle from the widow Casey, and by 1877 J. J. Dolan began efforts to swindle her out of the homestead she and Robert had worked for more than a decade to develop. In time John Chisum signed over the deed to the property he had acquired adjacent to the Casey place to Lily and a sister. Noted western historian Eve Ball, who edited the manuscript that was published as *My Girlhood Among Outlaws*, concluded that after the death of her husband "Mrs. Casey probably could not have survived without the help of John Chisum . . ." Lily kept a sheaf of letters to her mother from Chisum expressing "his desire to be as helpful as possible to us."[9]

As the Lincoln County War descended into murderous violence, Ellen Casey's friends persuaded her to return to Texas with her children until New Mexico was safer. During their two years in Texas, Ellen Casey took the opportunity to advance the education of her children. Lily was sent to Ursuline Academy in San Antonio, and she later became a teacher in New Mexico.

While the Caseys were in Texas, John Chisum erected a ranch house befitting a cattle king and a gracious host. By the time the Chisums returned from the Texas Panhandle with their cattle, the Square House had sustained considerable damage to plaster and to adobe walls. Indeed, some of the rooms had to be razed. It was an opportunity for Chisum to build a grand home,

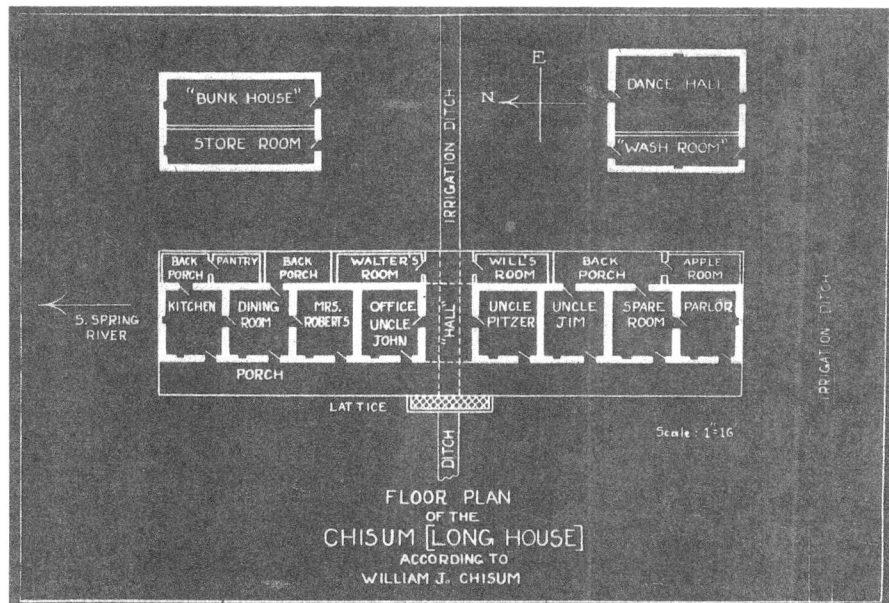

Floor plan of Chisum's spacious "Long House," which featured such luxuries as hardwood floors, glazed windows, expensive furniture, and Axminster carpets. Note the separate dance hall and the irrigation ditch which flowed beneath the open hallway. From a diagram by Will Chisum in the Chisum Files at the Haley Memorial Library.

and he seized the chance.

The new "Long House" was built 400 yards south of the old Square House. It faced west and was 144 feet long. There were eight spacious rooms, four on each side of a ten-foot wide open hall, beneath which an irrigation ditch flowed. A porch ran the length of the front side, and the rear porch extended along the east side. Soon, however, a great deal of the rear porch was enclosed, creating two additional bedrooms, a pantry, and an "Apple Room." The dining room, adjacent to the kitchen, featured a long table that seated twenty or more. The walls of the house were adobe, but the roof was gabled, with wooden shingles.[10]

Each of the eight original rooms had a door opening onto the front porch. John Chisum's room was on the left or north side of the hall, and a second door opened onto the hallway. His room was a combination office and bedroom. There was a heavy bedstead, a walnut desk, a safe, a big dictionary on an upright stand, chairs, and a carpet. Chisum enjoyed sitting on the front porch feeding breadcrumbs to fish in the spring water of the irrigation ditch.

A separate building about twenty feet behind the kitchen

John Chisum's "Long House."
JEH I.F 15.41. Courtesy Haley Memorial Library.

was a combination bunkhouse and store room. About fifty feet to the south was a large building that was used as a dance hall for dances and parties. Chisum did not want dancing on his fine Axminster carpets in the main house. Carpets, furniture, windows, shingles—all had to be hauled in 200 miles from the nearest railroad.

Chisum also imported hundreds of rose bushes, as well as shrubs and other flowers. He had two ponds scraped out, complete with an island that Pitser named the "Isle of Patmos." On the island the brothers planted three weeping willow trees, and elsewhere three cottonwood trees were planted. The cottonwoods "finally grew together—another symbol of their unity," according to Lily Casey Klasner. Chisum brought in "fruit trees of all sorts—apples, peaches, plums, pears, cherries, and nectarines," in addition to strawberries, raspberries, and blackberries. Two rows of cottonwoods framed the road to the Long House. The dirt scraped out for the ponds was packed into three mounds and covered with Bermuda grass, along with ornamental shrubbery. Steps led the way to the top of each of the three mounds, but also "typified the three Chisum brothers."[11]

Chisum's splendid frontier home was christened with a Christmas feast and dance in 1880. The big dining room table was loaded with baked turkey and ham, barbecued meat, fresh loaves of bread, cakes, pies, and other delicacies. The new dance hall behind the Long House was the scene of an all-night party. People came from miles away, dancing while John and Pitser fiddled and others played guitars. It was a memorable occasion for the Cattle King of the Pecos.

When the Casey family returned to Lincoln County, Lily frequently was invited to Chisum's impressive new ranch house. "I had . . . the good fortune to spend several months at the South Spring River ranch several times when it was in the height of its prosperity. During this time I often rode with Uncle John when he was making trips to look after his interests." During these trips Chisum spoke at great length with his teenaged companion. "Even now I do not exactly understand why he was inclined to talk to one so much younger in years in the free and full way he did . . . Sometimes I have thought that in those last years of his life, with so many perplexing things on his mind that he had to open up to someone, and I, being the one at hand, became the party of the second part in these conversations. Then, of course, I did not bother myself with the why's and wherefore's of the situation but felt myself honored, and I cherished in my heart all the words I could."[12]

Lily was profoundly impressed by Chisum's ranch home. "The Chisum ranch, as it was generally called, was known far and wide, and people came from everywhere to look at it. Uncle John always welcomed visitors and liked to conduct them all over it, explaining everything and describing other things he proposed to have done." She stressed that "Uncle John's hospitality was always generous and open handed, and everybody who came to the country stopped with him either for old acquaintance' sake or for the chance to see a remarkable man and a unique place, so the house was nearly always entertaining company."[13]

Life at the Chisum Ranch long remained an exciting memory for Lilly. "The ranch was always humming with activity. Uncle John, the general overseer and boss of it all, had shifted his interests from cattle raising to farming." He kept thirty Mexicans employed planting alfalfa in "the big field," a 500-acre irrigated field. His farm workers also planted trees, digging the holes and holding each tree upright while Chisum himself carefully shoveled the dirt "and tamped it firmly about the roots."[14]

Lily and other young people—including cowboys attracted to the girls—frequently enjoyed fishing. "The South Spring River in those days was very wide and deep, and as clear as crystal," she remembered. "It was filled with all sort of fish – catfish, sunfish, bull heads, suckers, eels, red horse, and buffalo

Chisum planted hundreds of irrigated acres in alfalfa.
JEH I.F 15.10. Courtesy Haley Memorial Library.

fish were all present in large quantities."

Chisum assigned Dwight Simms, "boss carpenter on the place," to build two rowboats. "Many and many were the rides we girls took . . . with the rowboats," reminisced to Lily. The smaller boat was kept in the oval pond for rides around the Isle of Patmos. There was a lot of singing of "the old-time songs" during boat rides. "What good times we had on the old ranch!" exclaimed Lily. "How happy everyone was, even though the section was crude and lawless!"[15]

Lily was impressed by the charity Chisum extended to his neighbors. "Uncle John was always furnishing poor people with supplies from his store . . ." Often Lily heard him instruct his hostess to "go to the store, pick up what you think they need, and have it sent over to them." Sometimes he sent clothing for threadbare children. Once he "bought a nice team of black horses and a wagon" and sent them to a widow with five children who had a farm but no wagon and team. Of course, Lily knew first-hand of Chisum's generosity for the kindnesses he extended to the Casey family.[16]

"Uncle John was a man of intense likes and dislikes," said

Lily. "One peculiarity was that he would not live in a two-story house. Neither would he stay in a second-story room for even a night if it could be avoided. When he went to a hotel in Las Vegas, or Santa Fe, or even in New York, he always insisted that his room be on the first floor." Chisum had a horror of both fire and stairwells, and if he could not be accommodated, "he never stayed more than one night, moving the next day to a hotel which could supply a room on the ground floor."[17]

"Uncle John enjoyed the company of ladies," emphatically stated Lily. "He liked greatly having with one or more of them a bantering conversation, full of jokes and raillery and even teasing, but he never descended to coarseness or roughness. He seemed especially to like ladies who were lively, jolly, and high strung, yet not inclined to sentimentality." Chisum once told Lily that that she was popular around the ranch because she was "the sort who scraps back" when teased. "It was this type," she concluded, "the sort that scraps back, that Uncle John enjoyed selecting for his lady friends."[18]

Lily's admiration for the cattle king who befriended her was enormous. "John Chisum was one of the men whom the Southwest should delight to honor," she said flatly. While researching and editing Lily Klasner's manuscript, Eve Ball heard it "rumored that had she so wished [Lily] could have married John Chisum."[19] But the age difference between John and Lily was nearly forty years. For Lilly, John Chisum probably represented a father figure instead of a sweetheart. The cattle king may have been a tough act to follow, however—Lily Casey married a fine-looking young man named Joe Klasner, but the marriage ended in divorce.

Sophie Aberdeen Poe was born in 1862, the same year as Lily Casey. Sophie's parents died when she was a child, and she and her younger sister went to live with an older married sister in Illinois. In 1881 Sophie accepted an invitation to join her older brother, Fred, in New Mexico. Fred was working near Roswell at the ranch of Capt. Joseph C. Lea. Sophie met the famous John Chisum at the Lea home, hearing his booming laugh before they were introduced. Sophie described him as "red-faced and hearty, a man of about sixty-five."[20] [He was fifty-seven.]

"Bless my heart!" cried Chisum. "So this is the little girl I've been hearing about? I am glad to meet you, my dear." Sophie "liked him instantly, as he held my small hand in a viselike grip." They talked about his new house, and Chisum asked her to come

John Chisum apparently considered proposing to Sue McSween, but soon retreated to the safety of bachelorhood. *Authors collection.*

for a week's visit. The next week Chisum drove his buggy to the Lea ranch to pick up Sophie. At dinner that night Chisum escorted her into the dining room, seated Sophie at his left, and jokingly began to call her, "Mrs. Chisum." During the week Sophie admired the hardwood floors, Axminster rugs, Chisum's "beautiful walnut desk," the curtains, the rose garden, and the peach orchard. Chisum told Sophie that the house, furnishings, and outdoor improvements cost him $20,000.

John and Sophie conversed freely, and there were daily invitations: "Mrs. Chisum, it's time for us to feed the fish." Chisum gave Sophie a horse so that she could visit South Spring in the future. At Thanksgiving in 1881 everyone "within a radius of seventy-five miles was invited" to an all-night dance. At Christmas Chisum gave Sophie "a pair of glittering bracelets," ordered from Merced & Jacquard in St. Louis. In 1883 Sophie married John W. Poe, Pat Garrett's deputy when Billy the Kid was killed. But like Lily Casey Klasner, she always admired Chisum's "strong, frank personality," his "remarkable business ability," and "his genial laugh."

Some young ladies were not charmed by Chisum. Mary V. Daniel, whose father was an army officer at Fort Stanton, was rankled by Chisum during his visits to their home. "John loved money," she concluded. "[He] was very dictatorial and was accused of 'cutting corners' when to his advantage." Mary decided that Chisum remained unmarried because "he was plain too hard to get along with."[21]

There was one woman who caused Chisum to waver in his lifelong commitment to bachelorhood. Like everyone else in and around Lincoln in the mid-1870s, he was struck by Sue McSween. In 1875 she moved with her husband, Alexander McSween, from Kansas to New Mexico Territory. Alex and Susan had married in 1874. He was an attorney, and the couple decided to settle in Lincoln, where Alex became the only lawyer in the county seat. Susan was an attractive woman with fashionable clothes and carefully groomed hairstyles. She was a musician with a vivacious personality, and she was one of the few Anglo women in town.[22]

Alex soon became a business partner with John

Sue McSween, the attractive and intelligent widow who eventually became the "Cattle Queen of New Mexico." *Courtesy Anderson–Freeman Museum, Lincoln Historic Site.*

Tunstall and John Chisum. When Chisum came to Lincoln he stayed at the hacienda-style residence of the McSweens. The McSweens sometimes stayed at the Chisum ranch, and as the Lincoln County War escalated Sue took refuge at South Spring. Chisum and the McSweens planned a trip together to escape the hostilities, but John and Alex were arrested before the trio could leave New Mexico. During the five-day Battle of Lincoln in July 1878 Susan courageously stayed in her besieged home even as the building burned. The women finally were evacuated, but Alex was killed during the climactic volleys. Attempting to salvage something tangible from the disaster, Sue McSween had herself appointed administrator of the estates of her husband, of John Tunstall, and of Dick Brewer.

Demonstrating an aptitude for business, she began to straighten out the tangled affairs of these men, even managing to recover some of the cattle stolen from the dead trio. Chisum provided Sue with monetary gifts and other assistance. Chisum gave her forty head of cattle as a starter herd, and soon she bought another 100 head from him. According to Sue, Chisum gifted her with a gold chain.[23] Chisum was impressed with her courage and intelligence, as well as with her looks and feminine style. Sue was twenty-one years his junior, which fit his customary pattern. After his twenties Chisum never showed interest in women his age. Chisum was fifty-five in 1879 and apparently the graying hair and wrinkles of a woman of his generation held little appeal for him.

Sue McSween had been a widow for a year when rumors began circulating around the ranch that the cattle king soon would propose. Sallie Chisum remembered when her uncle donned one of his business suits to visit Sue. "He wore his best handmade boots and Stetson hat." Sallie heard that her uncle had opened the subject of Sue becoming "the queen of the jinglebobs" when one of his cowboys rode up with news that he was trailing stolen cattle.

"Uncle John turned his horse around and joined him," related Sallie.[24] Perhaps Chisum was relieved at the arrival of a distraction, because he immediately broke off his matrimonial conversation and apparently never brought it up again. John Chisum retained the bachelorhood he was so comfortable with, while Sue worked hard and prospered as "New Mexico's Cattle Queen."

Chisum had the pleasure of female company at his South Spring headquarters in 1877 and 1878. When Hunter & Evans purchased 60,000 head of Jinglebobs, Col. Robert D. Hunter asked his brother David to travel to the Chisum ranch to represent the firm during the long roundup activities. David had charge of the firm's stockyards in Palestine, Texas, but he led a caravan of cowboys and supply wagons to New Mexico. David also brought his wife, Margaret, and his half-sister, Lizzie. At the end of the long journey they were welcomed at the Square House by John and Pitser Chisum, "who seemed glad to see us and showed such hospitality that we felt right at home with them," reported Margaret. "Mr. Chisum took us through his nice sitting room and office into two rooms prepared for us . . ." Margaret was impressed by the Mexican cook, and they dined at a long table in the big kitchen. "Mr. Chisum honored me by seating me at the head of the table, a place I occupied while we lived there."[25]

"Mr. Chisum introduced us to many of his friends," said Margaret, "[and] when not too busy he would chat with us." Margaret and Lizzie enjoyed meeting Sue McSween, who came to the ranch on business matters. "She was a fine, stylishly dressed, handsome lady." James Chisum arrived late in 1877 with his two sons and daughter Sallie, "a pretty, fair-haired girl, full of life and ready for any kind of sport. We spent many happy months together on the ranch."[26]

But the Hunters moved to Bosque Grande in mid-1878, because of the mounting violence of the Lincoln County War.

The old adobe house "was just about like living in a camp—bare rooms, no rugs, nothing to brighten the rooms." They set a clock on the mantle of a corner fireplace, along with a few family photographs "and a good picture of our friend John Chisum." Early one morning he drove up to Bosque Grande in a buckboard, evidently after an overnight journey. Following an exchange of greetings, Chisum ate breakfast, and he asked Margaret to prepare a box lunch for him. While he ate he recounted the sad details of the most recent violence in and around Lincoln. He said his goodbyes "with a sad smile." They expected to see him soon on our return trip, but Chisum spent the next year in the Texas Panhandle, while the Hunters completed the cattle transfer and left New Mexico. "We never saw him again."[27]

Margaret and Lizzie Hunter knew and liked Sallie Chisum. So did Sue McSween and Sophie Poe and Lily Casey Klasner—indeed Lily and Sallie lived together for a time in later years, hoping to collaborate on a book about John Chisum. Billy the Kid apparently had a crush on Sallie, and like many other cowboys he dropped by South Spring Ranch as often as possible hoping to see and perhaps talk with Chisum's niece.

Sallie Lucy Chisum was born in 1858, the second child of James and Ara Chisum. Sallie had an older sister, Mary (born in 1855), and two younger brothers,

Pretty Sallie Chisum served as her uncle's hostess at South Spring, and she became known as the "Queen of the Jingle-Bob." *Courtesy Artesia Chamber of Commerce.*

Walter (1861) and Will (1863). James stayed in Denton County, but Mary died in 1873, and Ara passed away two years later.

In 1877 James accepted John's invitation to move his family to the New Mexico operation. The long trek was arduous, but James and his party arrived at the Square House an hour before midnight on Christmas Eve. Exhausted, the travelers collapsed into bed without supper. John welcomed the family warmly, and it was easy to find work for the newcomers. Sallie was nineteen, lovely and lively and liked by everyone. She capably aided her uncle with the constant flow of visitors to South Spring.[28]

But the Lincoln County War became a homicidal conflagration during 1878, and Sallie found herself on another family trek, to the Texas Panhandle. They returned to South Spring in 1879, and John Chisum began building the Long House. Also in 1879 Sallie met William Robert, a German citizen who immigrated to America in 1873. By 1877 he had opened a store in Anton Chico, and business brought him to Roswell. Sallie married William Robert in Anton Chico in January 26, 1880, but John Chisum, in his paternalistic manner, employed Robert at South Spring as bookkeeper. Sallie continued to act as hostess at the Long House, and the popular young woman became known as "Queen of the Jinglebob" for the "Jinglebob King of the Pecos."

Chapter Nine

End of the Chisum Trail

*"I am now in a good fix for courting the
girls as I cannot speak above a whisper."*
—John Chisum

John Chisum had only a few years to enjoy his magnificent
new ranch estate and the baronial lifestyle of a famed cattle king. He enjoyed excellent health into his fifties. Chisum
displayed incredible physical stamina, on the range and on
long business trips, as well as at his walnut desk, composing a
blizzard of business correspondence. In 1877, at the age of fif-
ty-three, he was stricken with smallpox. "At one time it seemed
as his illness might prove fatal," recalled Lily Casey Klasner.
But a long convalescence at South Spring Ranch and his rugged
constitution provided a resilient recovery. "He thought the time
lost by the illness well spent for he seemed to have almost a
new body."[1]

It was fortuitous that Chisum bounced back so strongly.
The next two years were deeply stressful, as Lincoln County
was enveloped by the cauldron of all-out war. Both of Chisum's
partners in Lincoln, John Tunstall and Alexander McSween,
were among the murder victims, and the Cattle King of New
Mexico was unjustly held in captivity in Las Vegas. For a year
after his release the Chisums moved to the Texas Panhandle,
although John spent part of that time on a business trip to cities
with amenities.

Upon his return to South Spring he plunged into erecting

a splendid frontier residence. Once everyone moved into the Long House he focused upon creating a magnificent set of grounds, followed by irrigated farming in adjacent fields. There was even more visitor traffic than usual, as travelers came to South Spring to see the Cattle King's grand estate and to enjoy his legendary hospitality. Chisum proudly toured everyone through his lavishly furnished home and the surrounding estate. Newspaper reporters were among the visitors, and many were impressed by the improvement and growth of the cattle herd, so recently reduced after the removal of more than 50,000 head to Hunter & Evans. On April 3, 1833, the *Las Vegas Gazette* reported that:

> Uncle John S. Chisum, the pioneer cattlemen of the Pecos country, and who is reputed as having owned all the cattle in N. Mexico at one time, has recently imported from Clay County, Missouri, forty-two head of shorthorn Durhams—as fine animals as ever held down hoofs. The cattle cost him from $150 to $1500 . . .

A reporter from the *Denver Daily News* was similarly impressed, stating on April 11, 1883:

> One of the finest bunches of cattle in New Mexico is controlled by John S. Chisum . . . his herd numbers 30,000 head of the best graded cattle . . . Last year 6,000 calves were branded with the U on the shoulder, the distinguishing mark of the cattle king.

When Chisum brought Sophie Aberding Poe to his new ranch headquarters, she was taken aback by the luxuries she saw. "I was surprised to find the new house wonderfully modern in all its equipment and furnishings."

In the 1800s Chisum's South Spring Ranch clearly gave the impression that it remained the gigantic operation that once ran 200 miles along the Pecos River, supporting 60,000 to 80,000 head of cattle. But in recent years a great many settlers had arrived, clustering especially in the south, and also establishing homesteads elsewhere along the Pecos River and its tributaries to the west. To the north, Texas rancher George Littlefield bought the Bosque Grande property and buildings from a homesteader. Littlefield closed out his LIT operations in the Texas Panhandle, and sent Phelps White to New Mexico to establish a new LFD ranch.

Littlefield sent 9,000 head of cattle from Texas, and as calves failed along the way, the drovers joked that the new brand stood for "Left For Dead." Meanwhile, manager Phelps White was buying New Mexico cattle, from small bunches up to herds of 1,000. Soon cattle were grazing on an LFD range that measured forty by eighty miles. Although Chisum's cattle numbered at least 30,000, his range along the Pecos River had been reduced to sixty miles. Admittedly Chisum still managed a large operation. When Phelps White visited South Spring to buy bulls, he came away as impressed as the newspaper reporters and every-

The annual roundup was in progress when Chisum left to seek expert medical care in the East. Because it was such a busy time at the ranch, Chisum did not allow any family members to accompany him. At the end, however, he sent for brother James Chisum to come to his bedside. *JEH I.F 15.25. Courtesy Haley Memorial Library.*

one else. White wrote to a relative in Texas:

> I wish you could see old man Chisholms [*sic*] Ranch & cattle,
> the best in the Territory. His house cost him twelve thousand
> Dol All well fitted out, but the old man will have to leave soon
> as he is getting old.[3]

White's final statement was perceptive. Chisum was still in
his fifties, but health problems apparently had begun to affect
his appearance. By 1883 a tumor began to grow on his neck,
"and was operated on by local physicians for some time, and
with apparent success . . ." But when the growth reappeared he
expressed deep concern to Lily Casey, "because both his father
and grandfather had died from the same trouble, and he was
inclined to feel sure his was to be a similar fate." Chisum was
not in pain, "but the growth was so large and uncomfortable
on the left side of his neck, just over the shoulder, that to avoid
discomfort he had let his right shoulder sag down and incline
his head in that direction."[4]

Chisum did not like to talk about his obvious condition, and
he tried to carry on normal activities. He remained an active
member of the Lincoln County Stock Association, and Chisum
was one of 125 ranchers who attended the 1884 meeting of the
New Mexico Cattle Raisers Association in Santa Fe. Soon, however, "he decided to go get the best medical attention available,
and very quietly announced his determination to those of us
then at the ranch."

Chisum vaguely intended to go to Chicago or New York,
and he departed the ranch in his buggy on July 7, 1884. A roundup was in progress, and he asked family members not to go
with him at such a busy season. He was accompanied only by
a neighbor named Anderson, who traveled all the way with the
ailing cattle king. Chisum "seemed to feel a premonition that he
would never return," and he was visibly upset. "The rest of us
felt much the same way," said Lily, who wrote her sister "that I

felt I would never see Uncle John again."[5]

When Chisum reached Las Vegas he delayed his trip to the East long enough to take "part in an important conference of cattlemen concerning the locating of shipping pens in Bernal." Further attesting to his prominence as a cattleman, Chisum later was notified that he had been appointed a deputy commissioner to represent the range cattle industry at the Southern Industrial Exposition in New Orleans, commencing on December 1, and lasting into the spring of 1885. Chisum would have revelled in the New Orleans event, but the state of his health prevented his attendance.[6]

From Las Vegas, Chisum took the train to Kansas City, where he often had traveled on business. In Kansas City he consulted reputable physicians, "and finding that they took a serious view of his condition, he consented to an operation then and there at their hands." He arrived on July 16, abandoned any idea of traveling on to Chicago or New York, and submitted to surgery on July 24, 1884. On August 30, he wrote to Sallie Robert at South Spring. He told his niece that neighbor Anderson had returned to New Mexico, and he related that the tumor "was about the size of a beef's kidney. It was a very dangerous operation but it is over now and I am getting well and can leave for home in a week." Chisum added that "I regretted to leave home but was compelled to have this pet cut out. The doctor says if it had not been cut out it would have killed me in about six months more. He says it was the enlargement of the glands."[7]

Chisum finally felt strong enough to return to New Mexico, but by the time he reached Las Vegas, the malignant growth had returned and caused so much pain that he promptly headed back to Kansas City. The surgeon told Chisum he could not operate again until the patient was stronger.

On September 18, Chisum wrote to Lily Casey. Apparently it was the last letter he ever penned. He told Lily that "I would have written to you long ago but was so weak and poorly and it gave me so much pain to write I would put it off from time to time hoping I would feel better next day." Regarding the surgery, Chisum informed her that afterward he "was very weak, from the loss of blood having lost a bucket full, and was kept under the influence of chloroform for one hour." While attempting to build up strength for a second operation, "I am taking medicine by the wholesale and applying the battery [electrical treatments] twice per day." He was pessimistic about the next operation, since "I am much weaker . . ."

He could not resist a joking comment about an old subject: "I am now in good fix for courting the girls as I cannot speak above a whisper." Chisum closed this lengthy letter by assuring Lily that he thought of her "very often"—a sentimental note from a lonely, agonized man who was beginning to suspect that he was dying.

"I think of you as one of my very best friends and no one wishes you more happiness than I do. Do you think of me? I hope so. Don't write me as I am liable to go East."[8]

But Chisum did not go East. He did not go anywhere until December, languishing in his sickbed with no improvement. Physicians remained unwilling to attempt another surgery, and as Chisum's condition worsened, he was advised to seek relief at the new mineral springs resort being developed in Hot Springs, Arkansas.

There was an age-old—and slightly desperate—belief in the curative powers of mineral waters. "In classical Greece, waters with distinct tastes, smells, or colors often represented the abodes of gods and spirits," asserted Dr. Janet Valenza in her masterful history of the mineral springs and resorts in Texas. "People erected altars near sacred springs where they celebrated recovery by placing crutches, bandages, and replicas of diseased organs around their edges. Coins or small objects thrown into the waters served as supplication or gratitude."[9]

Romans founded hundreds of bathing establishments

throughout their vast empire. As many of these baths as possible were built where there were mineral waters, including, most famously, Bath in England. Temples and military hospitals were erected near these "sacred water sources." English colonists in America brought bathing traditions with them to the New World, where Native Americans already frequented mineral springs. During the 1700s Saratoga Springs in New York became America's best known mineral springs. In the South, many watering resorts were in rural areas. George Washington and Thomas Jefferson took the waters, and in the summers after the Civil War Robert E. Lee brought his family with him when he sought curative waters.

Springs form when surface water—rain or snow—seeps through pores and cracks in the soil into layers of rock. Finally reaching a layer through which it cannot pass, the water—now termed groundwater– collects underground until it finds a way through a crack or channel in the rock. Flowing to the surface, many of these springs contain minerals dissolved from rock by the moving water. Lampasas in the Texas Hill Country boasted seven mineral springs and became known as the "Saratoga of

Chisum traveled the last eighteen miles to Eureka Springs on a scenic new railroad spur. *Courtesy Eureka Springs Carnegie Public Library.*

Hotels and businessmen crowded the commercial district in 1883, the year before John Chisum arrived. *Courtesy Eureka Springs Carnegie Public Library.*

the South." But Eureka Springs had *sixty-six* springs that have been given names.

Eureka Springs is located in the Ozark Mountains in northwestern Arkansas, less than twenty miles south of the Missouri border. Native Americans long knew of the "Great Healing Spring" in the area, and after the Civil War word of the healing properties of the springs began to spread. Men and women struggled through the rugged countryside seeking curative powers for cancer, rheumatism, kidney disease, liver problems, sore eyes, asthma, ulcers, and even paralysis. At first they came by horseback or on foot, but soon stagecoaches traversed the widening trails. In 1880, Eureka Springs incorporated as a city, and tents rapidly gave way to more permanent structures. The Eureka Improvement Company was organized in 1882 to attract a railroad, and by 1883 an eighteen-mile spur was completed through the mountains. The Eureka Springs Railroad soon scheduled six trains each day, and the booming resort city became known as the "City Water Built" and the "Siloam of the Afflicted."

Late in 1884 a visibly afflicted John Chisum arrived at the frame depot of the Eureka Springs Railroad. Hotels were being built all over the hillside community, and Chisum would have checked in somewhere. Taking the waters included bathing in mineral springs and drinking large quantities of spring water. Health seekers went from spring to spring in the hills around Eureka Springs.

Lily Casey Klasner learned that Chisum submitted "himself to a course of baths and treatments that might prepare him for another operation." But he remained weak and uncomfortable. "Realizing the seriousness of his condition," Lily related, "he sent for Uncle Jim Chisum to come and be with him." A telegraph summoned James, and he came immediately by train. James was able to report on his older brother's last days. "For a time he seemed to improve at Eureka Springs, but about the middle of December, he grew rapidly worse."[10]

John Chisum was a pragmatic man of the frontier, and he confronted the fact that he was dying. As he contemplated a final resting place, Chisum rejected New Mexico Territory, where he had earned his greatest fame as a cattle king. He did not want burial in the state of his birth, because he left Tennessee when he was thirteen, en route to his first frontier. Chisum asked James to take him to Paris, his home from boyhood until thirty. He wanted to be buried beside his parents, Claiborne and Lucinda, in the family plot south of the Chisum home that teenage John had helped to build.

John Chisum died on Monday night, December 22, 1884. He had turned sixty the previous August, following surgery and in the midst of his struggle against cancer. James Chisum brought his brother's body to Paris by train. A large crowd assembled on Christmas Day for Odd Fellows burial rites administered by

Chisum probably took the waters at Basin Springs, label the "Balm of Life." *Courtesy Eureka Springs Carnegie Public Library.*

the Wildey Lodge.

There were numerous obituaries. *The Golden Era of White Oak* announced Chisum's demise on January 1, 1885:

> Our readers will be pained to learn of the death at Eureka Springs, Ark. of John S. Chisum, which occurred about two weeks ago. Mr. Chisum was one of the pioneers and frontiersmen of Lincoln County, having come here at a very early day and has been identified with the history ever since. Eccentric in many ways, gruff in manner, yet he was always a warm friend and no man ever looked closer after the pleasure and comfort of the men under

The impressive Chisum gravestone dominates the old hillside family cemetery in Paris. *Photo by the author.*

his employ during his long experience as a cattleman.

The Clarksville *Standard*, on January 9, 1885, focused on Chisum's younger years:

John S. Chisum, long known as one of the cattle kings, died at Eureka Springs on the 22nd . . . and was buried at Paris, Lamar County, . . . where the Chisum family lived in 1842, and where his father and mother died. When he came to Clarksville, John was the clerk of Wright & Montgomery, and was a merry hearted, laughing boy. Our last sight of him was in 1854 when he lived on the line of Cooke and Denton. Since then he had emigrated to New Mexico in pursuance of his owner of many thousand (head) of cattle. He was, we believe, never married. There are a few old residents of Clarksville who will remember John Chisum as he was in boyhood.

The Santa Fe *New Mexican* on December 31, 1884, described "New Mexico's pioneer cattle king" and his battle for health, "but the cancerous affection *(sic)* had planted a seed too deeply, and . . . Death proved victor . . . Chisum was the first range man in the territory and lived on the Pecos for many years. Last year he moved 10,000 head of his cattle to the San Simon country in Arizona, but his greatest interests are centered in New Mexico.

Closeup of gravestone information for John Chisum and his parents. *Photo by the author.*

He was a man greatly beloved by the early residents of Santa Fe and the territory in general. Peace to his ashes."

By the time that John Chisum was stricken with cancer, he and his ranching operation were under siege at the District Court of Lincoln County. Through the years numerous legal claims for damages had been pressed against Chisum, but he always proved elusive. Ten frustrated plaintiffs, through the prominent Santa Fe law firm headed by Thomas Catron, filed suit on April 24, 1884. More than $57,000 in damages were claimed against John, Pitser, and James Chisum, along with James's son-in-law, William Robert. But John was increasingly preoccupied by illness and avoided participation in the suit. On February 18, 1884, ten days before his fiftieth birthday, Pitser ended his bachelorhood, marrying Angie Isa Wells back in Lamar County, Texas. Pitser already had made a settlement with John for his long service, and he soon pulled out of New Mexico and spent the rest of his life in Paris.

After John's death, the remaining stockholders—James Chisum, his sons Walter and Will, and Sallie and William Robert—attempted to hold onto the Jinglebob Land and Cattle Company. But in the judgment of close observer Lily Casey Klasner, "they did not possess [John's] rare business ability. They tried to keep the business intact, but in spite of all that could be done, it began to drift slowly but surely toward the rocks." The Jinglebob Land and Cattle Company was lost to bankruptcy in the spring of 1891.[11]

None of John Chisum's successors at South Spring had either his leadership qualities or his affinity for cattle. But the frontier world of open range cattle grazing—the world in which Chisum had achieved such extraordinary success—disappeared at about the time the famous cattle king died. Chisum began his ranching career in 1854, at the dawn of the West's range cattle industry and with vast amounts of open range grazing available across the frontier. But the westward movement brought a relentless tide of settlers who acquired title to homesteads and made inroads into free grazing areas.

With the spirit of a true pioneer, Chisum continued to move west in search of more open ranges. But from the mid-1870s the appearance of barbed wire began to cut up rangelands, while overcrowding because of the cattle boom rendered pasturage thinner every year. The winter of 1885-86 was cold and blustery, and the torrid summer of 1886 withered grass and dried up streams. With weakened herds and grazing, the frigid winter of 1886-87 killed thousands upon thousands of cattle and finished the open range phase of the western ranching industry. Ranchers now had to fence their lands, restrict their herds to a manageable size, and provide winter feed by growing hay. The West became a land of big pastures, stocked with carefully bred beeves. The wide-open heyday of free-grazing empires was ended.

The career of John Chisum spanned the era of open range

ranching. His temperament and talents suited him perfectly for the frontier world of free grazing, and he put together three open range ranches, two in Texas and a massive spread in New Mexico. The Jinglebob ranch became the largest open range operation under a single rancher in the West, while Chisum for a time owned more cattle than any other man in America. There were those who envied Chisum, and those who were outright enemies. But he earned the respect and admiration of most of his peers. He was widely known as the Jinglebob King and the Cattle King of the Pecos and even the Cattle King of the West. And in cow country he certainly could have been dubbed the King of the Open Range.

Chapter Ten
Remembering a Cattle King

"There was land here for the taking and keeping if you were willing to fight — rustlers, disease, the land itself, Indians."

—John Wayne as Chisum telling
niece Sallie about early days in
New Mexico

In 1895, more than a decade after the death of John Simpson, a massive book was offered for sale: *Historical and Biographical Record of the Cattle Industry and the Cattlemen of Texas and Adjacent Territories.* The author was James Cox and he spent years compiling the book, which was more than 700 pages long, and each page was 8 ½ by 12 inches in size. Cox devoted almost 300 pages to a history of the range cattle industry, including sixty pages covering contemporary livestock commission firms and railroads. Cox and his biographical editor, S.D. Barnes, included 449 biographical sketches of cattlemen within 393 pages. The legendary Charles Goodnight commanded four pages, and Shanghai

John Wayne starred in Chisum in 1970.
Author's collection.

Pierce's bio covered nearly two pages. Goodnight and Pierce each had a bust illustration. Most of the other biographical sketches were compressed into less than a page.[1]

But the biographical section opened with a four-page article on John Simpson Chisum, which was preceded by a full-page image of a well dressed Chisum posing in a photographic studio. Although Chisum had died eleven years earlier, he was such a prominent figure in the western cattle industry that James Cox decided to feature him—front and center—in his massive book.

It was almost inevitable that the legendary cattle king would attract the greatest of all Western movie stars, John Wayne. *Chisum* was released in 1970, with Wayne in the title role. During filming of *Chisum* in Durango, Wayne received word that he had won the Best Actor Oscar for *True Grit*. Unfortunately, his portrayal of John Chisum was not Academy Award material.

Chisum was set during the Lincoln County War, and the familiar characters were present, including Billy the Kid, Pat Garrett, Sallie Chisum, John Tunstall, Alexander McSween, and Sue McSween. But John Wayne played John Chisum as John Wayne. There was little of the real Chisum in the movie character. There was a great deal of gunplay and other action, including stampedes and a brawl at the climax between Chisum and L.G. Murphy, played by Forrest Tucker. Throughout the movie Wayne's Chisum wears a gun rig, which the cattle king never did in real life. Chisum is a beautifully-filmed, action-packed Western, but it is a disappointment as a portrayal of

James Coburn gave a compelling portrayal of John Chisum in *Young Guns II*. *Author's collection.*

the colorful, complex Cattle King of the Pecos.

James Coburn provided a robust interpretation of Chisum in *Young Guns II*, a 1990 film about Billy the Kid and his gang and Pat Garrett. In one scene the Kid, played by Emilio Estevez, and four other outlaws ride up to Chisum's ranch house. Utilizing a familiar story as part of the plot, the Kid informs Chisum that he is owed $500 for his services as a gunman during the Lincoln County War. When Chisum ridicules the proposal, he is accused of stealing the farms of homesteaders, and the outlaws gun down two of his *pistoleros*. "I *am* New Mexico," growls Chisum, who soon pays Pat Garrett a bounty to track down the Kid.

Coburn earlier played Sheriff Garrett in *Pat Garrett and Billy the Kid*, a 1973 film which starred Kris Kristofferson as the Kid. Another fine actor, Barry Sullivan, was cast as John Chisum. But the director was the talented but mercurial Sam Peckinpaugh, and the plot went far astray. Among other disappointments, the part of Sullivan as Chisum was reduced to a cameo.

Other Chisum screen portrayals have been limited to a few minor movie and TV roles. Veteran character actor Roy Roberts played Chisum in *San Antone*, a 1953 Western that had no connection to real events. On television there was a John Chisum character in a 1960 episode of *Bronco* and in a 1965 episode of *Death Valley Days*.

If most of the movie and television characterizations of Chisum had been less than satisfactory, one motion picture presented a dynamic New Mexico cattle king with qualities clearly based on John Chisum. *The Furies*, a 1950 movie, was based on a 1948 novel of the same title written by best-selling author and screenwriter Niven Busch (who previously had penned *Duel in the Sun*). The central character is cattle king T.C. Jeffords, owner of a ranching empire in northeastern New Mexico Territory. Jeffords casually pays debts and wages and purchases in "T.C.'s", paper scrip bearing his initials. As the plot climaxes, his head-strong and ambitious daughter takes an extended business trip to buy up T.C.'s everywhere, at cents on the dollar. She arranges a major cattle purchase from her father, then pays him off with a chest full of T.C.'s. He roars with Chisum-style laughter, in a scene that emulates the IOU pay off supposedly made by Robert D. Hunter to the Cattle King of New Mexico. T. C. is flamboyantly played by a superb actor, Walter Huston, and Barbara Stanwyck plays his daughter. *The Furies* is a forgotten Western that offers the silver screen glimpses of a fascinating Chisum-like character.

There is no more important component to the public reservoir of memory about an historical figure then statuary. Statues are works of sculpture, which is one of the most complex and expressive of the arts. A small statue, usually little enough to be picked up, is known as a statuette or figurine. But one that

The Furies offered a dynamic performance by Walter Huston as a New Mexico rancher based on John Chisum. Barbara Stanwyck also was superb as his head-strong daughter. *Author's collection.*

A magnificent equestrian statue portrays Chisum herding a longhorn. This impressive sculpture was created by Robert Temple Summers and stands in Roswell's Pioneer Plaza. *Photo by the author.*

is larger than life size is called a colossal statue, and equestrian statues are especially impressive. Colossal statues usually are utilized as public art, commemorating historic individuals or events, and representing considerable investment.

John Chisum is the subject of a majestic equestrian statue that dominates Pioneer Plaza, across the street from the 1912 Chavez County Courthouse in Roswell. In 1999 the John Chisum Memorial Foundation commissioned sculptor Robert Temple Summers of Glen Rose, Texas, to create a statue of the Cattle King of the Pecos at 150 percent of life size. Presented to the public on March 24, 2001, the work features a vigorous Chisum, mounted and herding a longhorn. Summers executed a striking likeness of Chisum in his prime, and the statue group is a fitting public tribute to one of the most memorable figures of the range cattle industry of the Old West.

Summers promptly was commissioned to provide a sculpture of Sallie Chisum for Artesia, located just forty miles south of Roswell. Sallie Chisum Robert gave her husband three sons, although the first baby died at birth. But Sallie and William Robert separated in 1890 and divorced five years later. In that year, 1895, Sallie wed Baldwin Stegman. A new town, Stegman, was named after him, and Sallie became first postmistress in 1899. The name of the town later was changed to Artesia, while the Stegman marriage ended in divorce.

In 1889, while she was separated but not yet divorced from William Robert, Sallie established a home at Chisum Spring, an artesian well at the future town site. Chisum Spring had been used as a

Robert Temple Summers also sculpted Queen of the Jinglebobs, showing Sallie Chisum Robert reading to two children in Artesia. *Photo by the author.*

watering site for Jinglebobs for years, and in 1890 Sallie filed a homestead claim. In time she sold her acreage for town lots. Although Sallie's reputation suffered from two divorces and from her friendship with the outlaw Billy the Kid, she became known for taking in underprivileged children and seeing to their education.[1]

Robert Temple Summers created a large bronze statue of Sallie reading to two children. It stands on Artesia's Main Street and is titled, *First Lady of Artesia.* In 2012 Summers unveiled an equestrian statue of Pat Garrett near the courthouse in Roswell.

For those who wish to travel to the sites of Chisum's life, there are places where ghosts of the nineteenth century may be felt. The Great White House near Bolivar was expanded in the front before finally being taken down in recent years.[2] But a new home stands today at the commanding hilltop site selected by Chisum and road signs proclaim "Chisum Road" and "Jinglebob Lane." During the Texas Centennial Year of 1936, large stone historical markers were placed at numerous sites around the state—including the Bolivar ranch location.

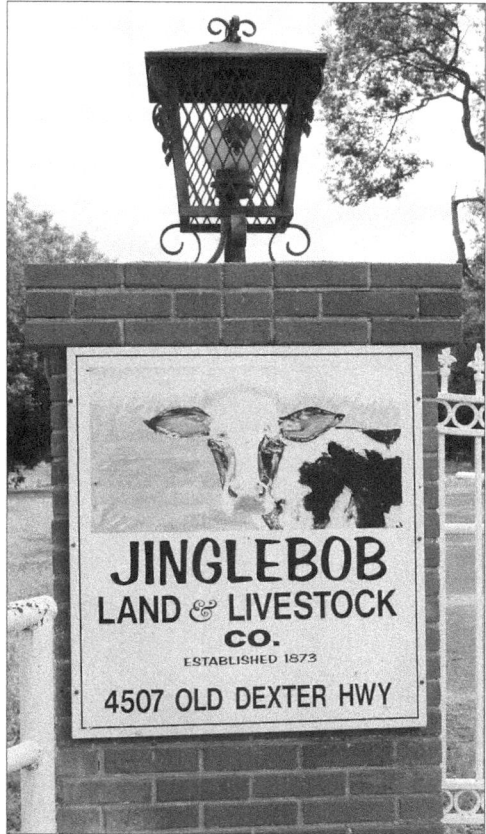

The famous South Spring property still is known as the Jinglebob Land & Livestock Co. *Photo by the author.*

At Trickham there also are historical markers, including a series of homemade signs honoring early settlers of the community. Just north of Paint Rock, seat of Concho County, another historical marker indicates the location—ten miles away on private property—of dugouts in the western area of Chisum's second ranch.

Lincoln, New Mexico, is the best preserved gunfighter town in the West. The single winding street now is paved, but most of the nineteenth-century structures still stand, including the historic two-story adobe built by L.G. Murphy, along with the Tunstall Store, where Chisum's bank was located. Chisum frequently visited Fort Stanton, which is ten miles from Lincoln

This 1936 historical marker was placed at Chisum's "Great White House," which still stood in expanded form. The stone erroneously lists the dates of Chisum's birth (August 16 instead of August 24) and death (September 22 instead of December 22). *Photo by the author.*

and well-preserved. Fort Sumner was devastated by flooding, but the ruins are informatively marked.

A beautiful headstone, as well as a historical marker, designates the peaceful gravesite of John Chisum and his parents in Paris. The family home stood to the north, but no traces remain. The Paris Public Library displays an original portrait of John Chisum. And just south of town is the campus of a rural consolidated school system, the Chisum Independent School District. The secondary school of the Chisum ISD, of course, is named Chisum High School, and the school mascot is the Mustangs.

Perhaps the most reassuring memory of John Chisum is the universal recognition I discovered during my research trips. When asked the subject of the book I was working on, there was immediate response to John Chisum. Often people thought of John Wayne's movie, Chisum, and many persons erroneously identified him with the Chisholm Trail. But even if they were fuzzy on details, almost everyone recognized his name, just as they would recognize Buffalo Bill Cody or Billy the Kid, Wyatt Earp

Near the first Chisum ranch headquarters at Bolivar is Chisum Road and Jingle Bob Trail. *Photos by the author.*

or Doc Holliday, Kit Carson or Charles Goodnight.

Cattle King John Chisum remains an iconic figure of the Wild West.

The campus of the Chisum Independent School District is located just south of Paris. *Photo by the author.*

Endnotes

Notes to Chapter 1

1. References to Chisum's nicknames are numerous. See, for example: Hinton, "John Simpson Chisum," *NMHR* , 185; *Grant County Herald*, Silver City, NM (April 11, 1875); Wallis, *Cattle King of the Staked Plains*, 43-53; Klasner, in *My Girlhood Among Outlaws*, constantly refers to "Uncle John" (who was not her uncle, but a man she respected and liked), and includes mention of "Old Chisum" on p.88; Clarke, *John Chisum, Jinglebob King of the Pecos*, 5, 7; Caldwell, *John Chisum, The Cattle King of the Pecos Revisited*, 61, 63, 158; Wallis, "Cattle Kings," *New Mexico* (July 1945), 21; *Santa Fe New Mexican*, obituary (December 31,1881).

2. "Family of Claiborne C. and Lucinda Armstrong 'Lucy' Chisum," Vertical File, Aiken Regional Archives, Paris, Texas; U.S. Census of 1830, Hardeman County, Tennessee.]

3. U.S. Census of 1830, Hardeman County, Tennessee; Hinton, "John Simpson Chisum," *NMHR* (July 1956), 185.

4. O'Neal, *Sam Houston*, 9-11.

5. Meacham, *Andrew Jackson*, 96.

6. Haley, *Charles Goodnight*, 235.

7. Klasner, *My Girlhood Among Outlaws*, 71, 236; Poe, *Buckboard Days*, 157-158.

8. Steely, *Forty Seven Years*, 380.

9. Harvill, "John Chisum Played Big Role in Developing the West," 2, John S. Chisum, Vertical File, Aiken Regional Archives, Paris, Texas.

10. Steely, *Forty Seven Years*, 380.

11. "Family of Claiborne C. and Lucinda Armstrong 'Lucy' Chisum," Vertical File, Aiken Regional Archives, Paris, Texas.

12. Ibid.; and Klasner, *My Girlhood Among Outlaws*, 233.

13. "Lamar County," Handbook of Texas, VI, 39-41; Stephens, Texas, *A Historical Atlas*, 136-137.

14. Klasner, *My Girlhood Among Outlaws*, 233.

15. Steely, *Forty Seven Years*, 380, 418; Caldwell, *John Simpson Chisum*, 31-32.

16. The story of "Tarrant's Expedition" is related in Allen, *Captain John B. Denton*, 130-139; "Village Creek, Battle of," *Handbook of Texas*, VI, 751; "Tarrant, Edward H," *Handbook of Texas*, VI, 206; "Denton, John Bunyard," *Handbook of Texas*, II, 598; "Battle of Village Creek," *Texas Sentinel*, (July 8, 1841).

17. Caldwell, *John Simpson Chisum*, 33-34.

18. Klasner, *My Girlhood Among Outlaws*, 238.

19. Klasner, *My Girlhood Among Outlaws*, 237, 238.

20. Chisum to James Vernon (September 29, 1851), located in Chisum, John S. Family, Vertical File, Aiken Regional Archives.

21. Klasner, *My Girlhood Among Outlaws*, 240.

22. Hinton, "John Simpson Chisum," *NMHR*, 181.

23. Captain J.M. Daniel was a friend of the Chisum brothers and hosted them in his home. His daughter, Mary, was a keen observer and developed strong opinions about the famous cattle king. Letter from May V. Daniel to Harwood Hinton (March 27, 1954), NMHR, 180.

24. "John Simpson Chisum," *Paris News* (October 10, 1937).

25. Klasner, *My Girlhood Among Outlaws*, 233.

26. Steely, *Forty Seven Years*, 484.

Notes to Chapter 2

1. "John Simpson Chisum," *Paris News* (October 10, 1937); Caldwell, *John Chisum*, 43.

2. Klasner, *My Girlhood Among Outlaws*, 234.

3. Steely, Forty Seven Years, 485; Klasner, *My Girlhood Among Outlaws*, 234.

4. Caldwell, *John Simpson Chisum*, 43,50, 143-151; Steely, *Forty Seven Years*, 487.

5. Klasner, *My Girlhood Among Outlaws*, 234; Clarke, John Chisum, 12,16; Steely, *Forty Seven Years*, 487.

6. The 100F placed a plaque on Chisum's gravestone proclaiming his membership.

7. Steely, *Forty Seven Years*, 485.

8. Harvill, "John Chisum Played a Big Roe in Developing the

West." John S. Chisum Vertical File, Aiken Regional Archives, Paris, Texas.

9. Allen, *Captain John B. Denton*, 130-147; Denton County Website; Steely, *Forty Seven Years*, 485.

10. Denton County Website; "John Simpson Chisum," *Paris News* (October 10, 1937).

11. "Bolivar, Texas," *Handbook of Texas*, I,

12. Caldwell, *John Simpson Chisum*, 48.

13. Caldwell, *John Simpson Chisum*, 161-164.

14. Steely, *Forty Seven Years*, 639.

15. "John Chisum," *Paris News* (October 10, 1937); Caldwell, *John Simpson Chisum*, 48-49.

16. Chisum to James Waide (March 7, 1862). Cited in Hinton, "John Simpson Chisum," *NMHR*, 186.

17. "Driskill, Jesse Lincoln," *Handbook of Texas*, II, 704; Klasner, *My Girlhood Among Outlaws*, 234.

18. Steely, *Forty Seven Years*, 487, 671.

19. Wallis, *Cattle Kings of the Stacked Plains*, 44.

Notes to Chapter 3

1. Haley, *Charles Goodnight*, 235.

2. Poe, *Buckboard Days*, 157-158.

3. Statement of Mrs. J. Smith Lea in regards to John Chisum, cited by Hinton, "John Simpson Chisum," *NMHR*, 180.

4. Caldwell, *John Simpson Chisum*, 45.

5. Caldwell, *John Simpson Chisum*, 51; Hinton, "John Simpson Simpson, *NMHR*, 187; Fridge, Ike Fridge, 5.

6. Fridge, *Ike Fridge*, 4.

7. Cox, "John Simpson Chisum," *Cattle Industry and Cattlemen of Texas*, 300.

8. Ibid.

9. Fridge, *Ike Fridge*, 6.

10. Caldwell, *John Simpson Chisum*, 45,76.

11. Fridge, *Ike Fridge*, 5.

12. *Ibid.*, 50; Hinton, "John Simpson Chisum," *NMHR*, 186.

13. Steely, *Forty Seven Years*, 672; Cox, "John Simpson Chisum," *Cattle Industry and Cattlemen of Texas*, 300.

14. Haley, *Charles Goodnight*, 121-122. J. Evetts Haley's classic biography of Goodnight was based considerably on extensive interviews with the old cattleman, who shed a great deal of light on John Chisum and the Goodnight-Loving Trail.

15. Haley, *Charles Goodnight*, 135.

16. Haley, *Charles Goodnight*, 134.

17. Haley, *Charles Goodnight*, 138.

18. Cox, "John Simpson Chisum," *Cattle Industry and Cattlemen of Texas*, 300; Caldwell, John Simpson Chisum,165, 169-170; Fridge, *Ike Fridge*, 16.

19. Cox, "John Simpson Chisum," *Cattle Industry and Cattlemen of Texas*, 300.

Notes to Chapter 4

1. Clarke, *John Chisum*, 21-22.

2. Redfield, "John Chisum Makes a Trail," *New Mexico Sentinel* (December 8, 1939).

3. Hinton, "John Simpson Chisum," *NMHR*, 188.

4. Klasner, *My Girlhood Among Outlaws*, 242.

5. Cox, "John Simpson Chisum," *Cattle Industry and Cattlemen of Texas*, 300.

6. Haley, *Charles Goodnight*, 204.

7. Haley, *Charles Goodnight*, 210.

8. Cox, "John Simpson Chisum," *Cattle Industry and Cattlemen of Texas*, 300.

9. Fridge, *Ike Fridge*, 12.

10. Hinton, "John Simpson Chisum," *NMHR*, 183.

11. Fridge, *Ike Fridge*, 14.

12. Fridge, *Ike Fridge*, 36-37.

13. Fridge, *Ike Fridge*, 4.

14. Haley, *Charles Goodnight*, 233.

15. Klasner, *My Girlhood Among Outlaws*, 245; Wallis, *Cattle Kings*, 48.

16. Fridge, *Ike Fridge*, 9.

17. Wallis, *Cattle Kings*, 48; Fridge, *Ike Fridge*, 40-41.

18. James P. Jones, Interview with J. Evetts Haley, January 13-14, 1927. Haley Memorial Library.

19. Cox, "John Simpson Chisum," *Cattle Industry and Cattlemen of Texas*, 301.

20. Fehrenbach, *Lone Star*, 560-561.

Notes to Chapter 5

1. Will Chisum submitted a diagram of the "Square House" on January 17, 1940, and it is located in a vertical file labeled "Chisum Ranches" in the Haley Memorial Library in Midland, Texas.

2. Quit Claim Deed to John Chisum, December 15, 1874. Copy in the Robert N. Mullin collection in the Haley Memorial Library: RNM, VI, CC-Chisum; Hinton, "John Simpson Chisum," *NMHR*, XXXI (July 1956), 189.

3. An extensive history of extralegal violence was presented by Richard Maxwell Brown in *Strain of Violence and Vigilantism*. Also see Frank Richard Parssel, *The Great American Outlaw, A Legacy of Fact and Fiction*; W. Eugene Hollon, *Frontier Violence, Another Look*; and Wayne Gard, *Frontier Justice*.

4. Brown, *Strain of Violence*, 59-60.

5. Brown, *Strain of Violence*, 95.

6. Cox, "John Simpson Chisum," *Cattle Industry and Cattlemen of Texas*, 301.

7. Wallis, *Cattle Kings of the Staked Plains*, 48-49.

8. Klasner, *My Girlhood Among Outlaws*, 248.

9. Cox, "John Simpson Chisum," *Cattle Industry and Cattlemen of Texas*, 301.

10. Klasner, *My Girlhood Among Outlaws*, 254; Coe, *Frontier Fighter*, 98-99; Hinton, "John Simpson Chisum," NMHR, 197; and Fulton, *Lincoln County War*, 37.

11. An earlier Chisum interview printed in *the Kansas City Livestock Indicator* (March 7, 1889), as cited in Hinton, "John Simpson Chisum," *NMHR*, 182.

12. Collinson, "The Chisum Ranches," *Ranch Romances*, 104-112.

13. English cowboy Frank Collinson related this story in his book, *My Life in the Saddle*, 141-142.

14. Erwin, Southwest of John H. Slaughter, 112-127; Klasner, *My Girlhood Among Outlaws*, 975-986.

15. A. M. (Gus) Gildea, "Experiences of a Trail Driver and Scout," *Trail Drivers of Texas*, 975-986.

16. Caldwell, *John Simpson Chisum*, 79.

17. Clarke, *John Simpson Chisum*, 49-50.

18. Deputy Sheriff Andy Boyle, report to U.S. Attorney T. B. Catron, June 15, 1877. Cited in Clarke, *John Simpson Chisum*, 52-55; Fulton, Lincoln County War, 37; Hinton, "John Simpson Chisum," *NMHR*, 198.

19. Cox, "John Simpson Chisum," *Cattle Industry and Cattlemen of Texas*, 302.

20. The story of the killing of "about 175" Indians on the Mescalero Reservation "not one mile from the post [Fort Stanton]" appeared in the otherwise authoritative biographical sketch by James Cox (see above citation). Chisum scholar Harwood Hinton accepted it.

21. Cox, "John Simpson Chisum," *Cattle Industry and Cattlemen of Texas*, 302.

22. Boyle Report to Catron.

23. Boyle Report to Catron.

24. Maurice G. Fulton to J. Evetts Haley (October 25, 1952), in John Chisum file at the Haley Memorial Library.

Notes to Chapter 6

1. Jimmy M. Skaggs in *The Cattle-Trailing Industry* provides over 300 accounts of trail drives by "cattle-trailing contractors," and his study "clearly shows that substantially more than half of the beeves driven to market in any given year were moved by people other than ranchers who had raised the animals." (p.11)

2. Cox, "John Simpson Chisum," *Cattle Industry and Cattlemen of Texas*, 300-301.

3. Caldwell, Robert Kelsey Wylie, 72-73; Cox, "John Simpson Chisum," *Cattle Industry and Cattlemen of Texas*, 301.

4. Hinton, "John Simpson Chisum," *NMHR*, 198;

5. Hinton, "John Simpson Chisum," *NMHR*, 183.

6. Clarke, *John Simpson Chisum*, 47.

7. Brothers, *A Pecos Pioneer*, 49.

8. Klasner, *My Girlhood Among Outlaws*, 143.

9. Hinton, "John Simpson Chisum," *NMHR*, 181.

10. Hinton, "John Simpson Chisum," *NMHR*, 182.

11. Collinson, "The Chisum Ranches," *Ranch Romances*, 112

12. Caldwell, *John Simpson Chisum*, 47, 72.

13. In January 1878 Chisum, who was incarcerated in Las Vega over the matter, wrote a lengthy account of his unwanted association with Wilber and Clark: "HOW I WAS IMPRISONED *AND FOR WHAT.*" A typescript is in the Haley Memorial Library in Midland, Texas.

14. Chisum, "HOW I WAS IMPRISONED," typescript, 2-3.

15. Chisum, "HOW I WAS IMPRISONED," typescript, 3.

16. Chisum, "HOW I WAS IMPRISONED," typescript, 4-6.

17. Grant County Herald, Silver City (April 11, 1876).

18. Collinson, *Life in the Saddle*, 143.

19. Collinson, *Life in the Saddle*,144; Collinson, "The Chisum Ranches," *Ranch Romances*, 108, 110.

20. Hinton, "John Simpson Chisum," *NMHR*, 184.

21. *Las Vegas Gazette* (November 15, 1875).

22. Clarke, *John Simpson Chisum*, 26.

23. Coe, *Frontier Fighter*, 98.

24. *Grant County Herald*, Silver City (April 11, 1876).

25. Accounts of the massive livestock sale to Hunter, Evans & Co. are in: Cox, "John Simpson Chisum," *Cattle Industry and Cattlemen of Texas*, 302; McLean, From Ayr to Thurber; Klasner, *My Girlhood Among Outlaws*, 253-254; Hinton, "John Simpson Chisum," NMHR, 190-191; Clarke, *John Simpson Chisum*, 32-36; Caldwell, *John Simpson Chisum*, 72-75.

26. Robert D. Hunter testimony, Rosenthal *et.al* vs. John Chisum, District Court of Lincoln, March 26, 1879; Hutchinson, "Old Jinglebob and the Legal Rustle," *Zane Grey Magazine*, 134-138.

27. Cox, "John Simpson Chisum," *Cattle Industry and Cattlemen of Texas*, 302.

Notes to Chapter 7

1. Keleher, *Violence in Lincoln County*, 51-53; Nolan, *Lincoln County War*, 32-37, 41-47, 496-497.

2. Beck, *New Mexico*, 163.

3. Beck, *New Mexico*, 164.

4. Cox, "John Simpson Chisum," *Cattle Industry and Cattlemen of Texas*, 302.

5. Clarke, *John Chisum*, 72-73.

6. Coleman, "J. K. Milwee, Frontiersman," *Frontier Times*, February 1937.

7. *Mesilla Independent* (August 18 and September 8, 1877)

8. Coe, *Frontier Fighter*, 25.

9. Chisum, "HOW I WAS IMPRISONED *AND FOR WHAT*." Las Vegas, January 16, 1878. Letters from Chisum to Ash Upson (January 21, 1878); to Ash Upson, Marion Turner, and Jim Jones (January 28, 1878); and to Ash Upson (January 31, 1878).

10. Nolan (ed.), *John Henry Tunstall*, 354.

11. Keleher, *Violence in Lincoln County*, 33-35, 60-63, 76-80, 253, 270-272; Rickards, *Gunfight at Blazer's Mill*, 14-15.

12. Florencio Chavez to J. Evetts Haley (August 15, 1972). FIles, Panhandle-Plains Library, Canyon, Texas.

13. Keleher, *Violence in Lincoln County*, 82-83; Hunt, *Tragic Days of Billy the Kid*, 39.

14. For an excellent account see Rickards, *Gunfight at Blazer's Mill*.

15. Coe, *Frontier Fighter*, 97, 103-105.

16. Hinton, "John Simpson Chisum," *NMHR*, 317.

17. Coe, Frontier Fighter, 137-139.

18. McCarty, *Maverick Town*, 41-42; Clarke, *John Simpson Chisum*, 102-103.

19. Hinton, "John Simpson Chisum," *NMHR*, 327.

20. Cox, "John Simpson Chisum," *Cattle Industry and Cattlemen of Texas*, 302.

21. Hinton, "John Simpson Chisum," *NMHR*, 333.

Notes to Chapter 8

1.   Klasner, *My Girlhood Among Outlaws*, 238.

2.   Interview With Dorothy Bramblett, November 19, 2017

3.   Caldwell, *John Simpson Chisum*, 43-44, 143-145.

4.   Caldwell, *John Simpson Chisum*, 172-176.

5.   Caldwell, *John Simpson Chisum*, 44, 85-86.

6.   Klasner, *My Girlhood Among Outlaws*, 230.

7.   Klasner, *My Girlhood Among Outlaws*, 70-72.

8.   Klasner, *My Girlhood Among Outlaws*, 72.

9.   Klasner, *My Girlhood Among Outlaws*, 3, 230, 316.

10. Floor Plan of the Chisum [Long House] according to William J. Chisum, on file in the Haley Memorial Library.

11. Klasner, *My Girlhood Among Outlaws*, 298.

12. Klasner, *My Girlhood Among Outlaws*, 230.

13. Klasner, *My Girlhood Among Outlaws*, 300-301.

14. Klasner, *My Girlhood Among Outlaws*, 302.

15. Klasner, *My Girlhood Among Outlaws*, 303-305.

16. Klasner, *My Girlhood Among Outlaws*, 315-316.

17. Klasner, *My Girlhood Among Outlaws*, 326-327.

18. Klasner, *My Girlhood Among Outlaws*, 318.

19. Klasner, *My Girlhood Among Outlaws*, 6, 229.

20. Poe, *Buckboard Days*, 157-165.

21. Hinton, "John Simpson Chisum," *NMHR*, 180,181.

22. See Kathleen P. Chamberlain's biography of Sue, *In the Shadow of Billy the Kid*, Susan McSween and the Lincoln County War.

23. Chamberlain, *In the Shadow of Billy the Kid*, 155, 163, 169, 172, 187.

24. Clarke, *John Simpson Chisum*, 115.

25. McLean, *From Ayr to Thurber*, 73-75, 80-81.

26. McLean, *From Ayr to Thurber*, 81-85.

27. McLean, *From Ayr to Thurber*, 86-87.

28. See: Turk and Robert, "Much Misunderstood Miss Chisum," *Wild West* (January 2018), 52-57; Caldwell, *John Simpson Chisum*, 10, 22, 44, 85, 118, 152-61, 163, 210; Knorr, "Queen of the Jingle-Bob," *True West* January-February, 1971), 14-16, 64-67; Clarke, *John Chisum*, 70, 72, 82, 110, 111, 112, 114-116, 119, 132, 135.

Notes to Chapter Nine

1. Klasner, *My Girlhood Among Outlaws*, 167-168.
2. Poe, *Buckboard Days*, 160.
3. Haley, *George W. Littlefield, Texan*, 137-141.
4. Klasner, *My Girlhood Among Outlaws*, 308-309.
5. Klasner, *My Girlhood Among Outlaws*, 308-309.
6. Cox, "John Simpson Chisum," *Cattle Industry and Cattlemen of Texas*, 302; Hinton, "John S. Chisum," *NMHR*, 65.
7. Klasner, *My Girlhood Among Outlaws*, 309-310.
8. Klasner, *My Girlhood Among Outlaws*, 310.
9. Valenza, *Taking the Waters in Texas*, 17.
10. Klasner, *My Girlhood Among Outlaws*, 310.
11. Klasner, *My Girlhood Among Outlaws*, 311-14.

Notes to Chapter Ten

1. Knorr, "Queen of the Jingle-Bob," *True West* January-February, 1971); Turk and Robert, "Much Misunderstood Miss Chisum," *Wild West* (January 2018).
2. Judge Tom Crum of Granbury, Texas, frequented the old house—which belonged to relatives—in his youth, and hunted the surrounding land. Tom shared memories of the historic location with me while this book was in progress.

Bibliography

There are three especially rich collections pertaining to John S. Chisum. Dr. Harwood P. Hinton amassed Chisum material for half a century, and eighteen boxes of his materials have been donated to the Southwest Collection at Texas Tech University. The Aikin Regional Archives at Paris Junior College has assembled a vast amount of material on Chisum and his family, and these items are carefully arranged in vertical files. J. Evetts Haley was an indefatigable interviewer and collector of cow country documents and clippings, and part of his legacy is an enormous Chisum collection, including archival photographs, at the Haley Memorial Library and Museum in Midland, Texas. Other items which I found useful are listed below.

Documents And Legal Documents

Lamar County District Court records. Paris, Texas.
Lincoln County District Court records. Lincoln, New Mexico.
Lamar County, County Clerk records, 1852-1854. Paris, Texas
Federal Census Records:
> Hardeman County, Tennessee: 1830
> Lamar County, Texas: 1850, 1860.
> Lincoln County, New Mexico: 1870, 1880.
Quit Claim Deed to John S. Chisum, from James Patterson.
> December 15, 1874, Lincoln County, New Mexico.
Chisum, John S. Brand Markings, Lamar County, Texas, August 1852.
Rosenthal, William, *et .al,* vs. John, James, and Pitser
> Chisum. District Court of Lincoln, 1884. Trial booklet.

Newspapers

Clarksville (TX) *Standard*
El Paso Times
Fort Worth Star
Mesilla Valley (CNM) *Independent*
Santa Fe New Mexican
Denton (TX) *Record-Chronicle*
Fort Worth Press
Grant County (NM) *Herald*
Paris News
White Oaks (NM) *Golden Era*

Books

Adams, Clarence S., and Tom E. Brown, Sr. *Three Ranches West, A True Story of John S. Chisum, The Cowman Who Opened the West for Cattle Trade.* New York: Caxton Press, Inc., 1972. 589 pp!

Adams, Clarence Siringo. *For Old Times' Sake*. Roswell, N.M.: Hall-Poorbaugh Press, Inc., 1980.

Allen, William. Captain John B. Denton, *Preacher, Lawyer, and Soldier, His Life and Times in Tennessee, Arkansas, and Texas*. Chicago: R.R. Donnelley & Sons Company, 1905.

Alexander, Bob. *Lawmen, Outlaws, and S.O.Bs. Gunfighters of the Old West*. Silver City, N.M.: High Lonesome Press, 2004.

Ballow, Willard. *Billy the Kid, A Graphic History*. Fort Worth: Owlhoot Trail Publishing Company, 1998.

Bates, Edmond Franklin. *History and Reminiscences of Denton County*. N.p., n.d.

Bogener, Stephen. *Ditches Across the Desert, Irrigation in the Lower Pecos Valley*. Lubbock: Texas Texas University Press, 2003.

Brothers, Mary Hudson. *A Pecos Pioneer*. Albuquerque: University of New Mexico Press, 1943.

Brown, Richard Maxwell. *Strain of Violence, Historical Studies of American Violence and Vigilantism*. New York: Oxford University Press, 1975.

Bryan, Howard. *Wildest of the Wild West*. Santa Fe: Clear Light Publishers, 1991.

Busch,Niven. *The Furies*. New York: The Dial Press, 1948.

Caldwell, Clifford R. *John Simpson Chisum, The Cattle King of the Pecos Revisited*. Santa Fe, NM: Sunstone Press, 2010.

Caldwell, Clifford R. Robert Kelsey Wylie, *Forgotten Cattle King of Texas*. Privately printed, 2012.

Chamberlain, Kathleen P. *In the Shadow of Billy the Kid, Susan McSween and the Lincoln County War*. Albuquerque: University of New Mexico, 2013.

Clarke, Mary Whatley. *John Simpson Chisum, Jinglebob King of the Pecos*. Austin: Eakin Press,1984.

Coan, Charles F. *A History of New Mexico*, Vol. I. Chicago and New York: The American Historical Society, Inc., 1925.

Coe, George W. *Frontier Fighter*, Albuquerque: University of New Mexico Press, 1934.

Collins, Frank. *Life in the Saddle*, edited by Mary Whatley Clarke. Norman: University of Oklahoma Press, 1963.

Cox, James. *Historical and Biographical Record of The Cattle Industry and the Cattleman of Texas and Adjacent Territory 1895*. St. Louis: Woodward and Tiernan Printing Co., 1895.

Cramer, T. Dudley. *The Pecos Ranchers In the Lincoln County War*. Oakland, California: Branding Iron Press, 1996.

Danielson, Kay Marnon. *Eureka Springs, Arkansas*. Charleston, S.C.: Arcadia Publishing, 2001.

Erwin, Allen A. *The Southwest of John H. Slaughter, 1842-1922*. Glendale, Calif: Arthur H. Clark Company, 1965.

Eureka Springs Carnegie Public Library Association. *Eureka Springs, A Pictorial History*. 2010.

Fehrenbach, T.R. *Lone Star, A History of Texas and the Texans*. New York: The Macmillan Company, 1968.

Fridge, Ike. *History of the Chisum War; or, Life of Ike Fridge. Stirring Events of Cowboy Life on the Frontier*. As told to Jodie D. Smith. Electra, Texas: J.D. Smith, 1917.

Gard, Wayne. *Frontier Justice*. Norman: University of Oklahoma Press, 1949.

Garrett, Pat. F. *The Authentic Life of Billy the Kid*. Norman: University of Oklahoma Press, 1954.

Haley, J. Evetts. *Charles Goodnight, Cowman and Plainsman*. Norman: University of Oklahoma Press, 1949.

Haley, J. Evetts. *George Littlefield, Texan*. Norman: University of Oklahoma Press,1943.

Halsell, H.H. *Cowboys and Cattleland*. Dallas: Williamson Printing Co., 1945.

Hollon, W. Eugene. *Frontier Violence, Another Look*. New York: Oxford University Press, 1974.

Hoyt, Henry F. *A Frontier Doctor*. Boston: Houghton-Mifflin Co., 1929.

Jenson, Joan M., and Darlis A. Miller. *New Mexico Women: Intercultural Perspectives*. Albuquerque: University of New Mexico Press, 1986.

Jordan, Terry G. *North American Cattle-Ranching Frontiers*. Albuquerque: University of New Mexico Press, 1993.

Kelcher, William A. *Violence in Lincoln County, 1869-1881*. Albuquerque: University of New Mexico Press, 1957.

Klasner, Lily. *My Girlhood Among Outlaws*, edited by Eve Ball. Tucson: University of Arizona Press, 1972.

McLean, William Hunter. *From Age to Thurber, Three Hunter Brothers and the Winning of the West*. Fort Worth Genealogical Society: New Printing Co.,1971.

Meacham, Jon. *Andrew Jackson, An American Populist*. New York: Time Inc. Books, 2017.

Meadows, John P. *Pat Garrett and Billy the Kid as I Know Them, Reminiscences of John P. Meadows*. Albuquerque: University of New Mexico Press, 2004.

Mullin, Robert N. *Maurice Garland Fulton's History of the Lincoln County War*. Tuscon: University of Arizona Press, 1984.

Nolan, Frederick. *The Lincoln County War, A Documentary History*. Norman: University of Oklahoma Press, 1992.

Nolan, Frederick. *The West of Billy the Kid*. Norman: University of Oklahoma Press, 1998.

O'Neal, Bill. *Henry Brown, The Outlaw Marshal*. College Station, Texas: Creative Publishing Company, 1980.

O'Neal, Bill. *Historic Ranches of the Old West*. Austin: Eakin Press, 1997.

O'Neal, Bill. *Sam Houston, A Study in Leadership*. Fort Worth: Eakin Press, 2016.

Padgitt, Jane. *A History of Coleman County and Its People*, Vol. I. The Coleman County Historical Commission, n.d.

Poe, Sophie A. *Buckboard Days*, edited by Eugene Cunningham. Caldwell, Idaho: Caxton Printers, 1936.

Potter, Jack. *Lead Steer and Other Tales*. Clayton, N.M.: The Leader Press,1939.

Prassel, Frank Richard. *The Great American Outlaw: A Legacy of Fact and Fiction*. Norman: University of Oklahoma Press,1993.

Prose and Poetry of the Livestock Industry of the United States, With Outlines of the Origin and Ancient History of Our Live Stock Animals. Prepared by Authority of the National Live Stock Association. Kansas City, 1915.

Rasch, Philip J. *Warriors of Lincoln County*. Edited by Robert K. Debarment. Stillwater, Oklahoma: National Association for Outlaws and Lawmen History, Inc., 1998.

Rickards, Colin. *The Gunfight at Blazer's Mill*. El Paso: Texas Western Press, 1974.

Skaggs, Jimmy M. *The Cattle-Trailing Industry, Between Supply and Demand, 1866-1890*, Norman: University of Oklahoma Press,1973.

Stephens, A. Ray. Cartography by Carol Zuber-Mallison. *Texas, A Historical Atlas*. Norman: University of Oklahoma Press, 2010.

Terry, Julia and Ralph (eds). *A History of Coleman County and Its People*, Vol. I. San Angelo: Coleman County Historical Commission,1985.

Twitchell, Ralph Emerson. *The Leading Facts of New Mexican History*, Vol. III. Cedar Rapids, Iowa: The Torch Press, 1917.

Utley, Robert M. *Billy the Kid, A Short and Violent Life*. Lincoln: University of Nebraska Press,1989.

Utley, Robert M. *Four Fighters of Lincoln County*. Albuquerque: University of New Mexico Press,1986.

Valenza, Janet Mace. *Taking the Waters in Texas: Springs, Spas, and Fountains of Youth*. Austin: University of Texas Press, 2000.

Wallace, Lew. Lew Wallace, *An Autobiography*, 2 Vols. New York and London: Harper & Brothers Publishers, 1906.

Wallis, George A. *Cattle Kings of the Staked Plains*. Dallas: American Guild Press, 1957.

Wallis, Michael. *Billy the Kid, The Endless Ride*. New York and London: W. W. Norton & Company, 2007.

Wellman, Paul I. *The Trampling Herd*. New York: Doubleday and Co., 1951.

Wilson, John P. *Merchants, Guns & Money, The Story of Lincoln County and Its Wars*. Santa Fe: Museum of New Mexico Press, 1987.

Articles

"The Battle of Village Creek." *The Texas Sentinel*. July 8, 1841.

Coleman, Max W. "J. K. Milwee, Frontiersman," *Frontier Times*, February 1937.

Collins, Frank. "Chisum Ranches." *Ranch Romances*. December 1936, 104-113.

Frazier, Donald S. "Village Creek, Battle of." *Handbook of Texas*, Vol. 6, 751.

Gray, Eunice Sullivan. "Bolivar, Texas." *Handbook of Texas*, Vol. I, 626.

Haight, Pete. "Herd 'Em Up, Move 'Em Out." *Texas Highways* (March 1975), 6-9.

Hinton, Harwood P., Jr. "John Simpson Chisum, 1877-84." *New Mexico Historical Review*, vol. XXXI, no. 3 (July 1956) and no. 4 (October 1956) and vol. XXXII, no. 1 (January 1957).

Hoole, W. Stanley. "Denton, John Bunyard." *Handbook of Texas*, Vol. 2, 598.

Hutchinson, W. H. "Old Jinglebob and the Legal Rustle." *Zane Grey's Western Magazine*. June 1949, 134-138.

"John Chisum Makes a Trail," *New Mexico Sentinel*, December 8, 1939.

Tidwell, Deb. "The History of Mules." *True West*, April 2017.

Knorr, Ruth. "Queen of the Jingle-Bob." *True West*. January-February 1971,14-16, 64, 66-67.

Laughlin, Charlotte. "Trickham, Texas." *Handbook of Texas*, Vol. 6, 563.

Lederman, Michael M. "Lamar County." *Handbook of Texas*, Vol. 4, 39-41.

Odom, E. Dale. "John Simpson Chisum, Denton Pioneer In World of Cattle." *Denton Record-Chronicle*, January 7, 1976.

Odom, E. Dale. "John Simpson Chisum, Denton Pictures In World of Cattle." *Denton Record-Chronicle*, January 7, 1976.

Page, Jake. "Was Billy the Kid a superhero - or a superscoundrel?" *Smithsonian*, February 1991, 137-146.

Potter, Jack. "The Jingle-Bob Brand." *New Mexico*. July 1945, 21, 35, 39.

Price, B. Byron. "Don't Fence Me In: The Range Cattle Industry in the Confederate Southwest, 1861-1865." *Southwestern Cattle Industry*.

Redfield, Georgia B. "John Chisum, 'Cattle King of Pecos Valley,' Born 129 Years Ago." *El Paso Times*, August 16, 1953.

Redfield, Georgia B. "John Chisum Makes a Trail," *New Mexico Sentinel*, December 8, 1939.

Robinson, Sherry. "Horsehead Crossing on the Pecos." *Wild West*. February 2017, 46-51.

Sinclair, John L. "On the Hoof." *New Mexico*. October 1939, 26-27, 42-43.

"Tarrant, Edward H." *Handbook of Texas*, Vol. 6, 206.

Wallis, George A. "Cattle Kings." *New Mexico*. June 1936, 26-27, 46-47.

Walsh, Mary Jayne. "Driskill, Jesse Lincoln." *Handbook of Texa*s, Vol. 2, 704.

Willis, Delbert. "A Great Cattle King, Defendants of John Chisum Live in Tarrant." *Fort Worth Press*. October 6, 1963.

Miscellaneous

Barber, Susan Mcsween. Interview with J. Events Haley, August 16, 1927. Haley Memorial Library.

Chisum, John S. "How I Was Imprisoned and *For What.*" Typescript of Chisum manuscript. Hinton papers, Southwest Collection, Texas Tech University.

Chisum, John S. Letter to James Vernon, September 29, 1851. Vertical File, Aikin Regional Archives, Paris Junior College.

Family of Claiborne C. and Lucinda Armstrong "Lucy" Chisum, Vertical File, Aikin Regional Archives, Paris Junior College.

Goodnight, Charles. Interview with J. Evetts Haley, November 13, 1926. Haley Memorial Library.

Harvill, Daisy. *John Simpson Chisum*. Pamphlet.

Jones, James P. Interview with J. Evetts Haley, January 13-14, 1927, Jones Ranch, Rocky Arroyo, N.M. Haley Memorial Library.

Nelson, Morgan. "James (Jim) Patterson, 1833-1892." Unpublished manuscript in Hinton papers, Southwest Collection, Texas Tech University.

Quit Claim Deed to John S. Chisum, from James Patterson. December 15, 1874, Lincoln County, New Mexico.

Steely, Skipper. *Forty Seven Years*. Paris: Northeast Texas Historical Preservation Association In Cooperation with the Wright Press, 1988. Bound volume.

Motion Pictures

Chisum (1970)   *Forty Guns* (1957)
The Furies (1950)   *Pat Garrett and Billy the Kid* (1973)
San Antone (1953)   *Young Guns II* (1990)

Index

Author Bio

Bill O'Neal currently is serving his sixth year as State Historian of Texas. As an ambassador for Texas history, Bill travels constantly across the Lone Star State, providing programs at schools and universities and a variety of historical events. He is a past president and fellow of both the West Texas Historical Association and of the East Texas Historical Association.

Bill is the author of more than forty books, as well as 300 articles and book reviews. His most recent writing award, the A. C. Greene Literary Award, was presented at the 2015 West Texas Book Festival in Abilene. In 2012 Bill received the Lifetime Achievement Award of the Wild West Historical Association, and in 2007 he was named *True West Magazine's* Best Living Non-Fiction Writer.

Bill has appeared on TV documentaries on TBS, The History Channel, The Learning Channel, CMT, A&E, and the American Heroes Channel Series, *Gunslingers*. During a long career at Panola College in Carthage, Texas, his most prestigious teaching award was a Piper Professorship, presented in 2000. In 2013 Panola's new dormitory was named Bill O'Neal Hall, and in that same year he received an honorary Doctor of Letters degree from his alma mater, Texas A&M University at Commerce. Bill's four daughters all have entered the field of education, and he is the proud grandfather of seven grandchildren

More Titles from Bill O'Neal & Eakin Press

The Arizona Rangers - 9780890156100 . . . . $19.95

The American Association
A Baseball History, 1902-1991 - 978-0890158128 . . . . $24.95

The Bloody Legacy of Pink Higgins:
A Half Century of Violence in Texas - 9781571683045 . . . . $19.95

Border Queen Caldwell
Toughest Town on the Chisholm Trail - 9781934645666 . . . . $24.95

Captain Harry Wheeler, Arizona Lawman - 9781571680648 . . . . $21.95

Cattlemen Vs Sheepherders
Five Decades of Violence in the West - 9781571688569 . . . . $22.95

Cheyenne: 1867 to 1903:
A Biography of the Magic City of the Plains - 9781571688392 . . . . $29.95

Doris Miller-Hero of Pearl Harbor - 9781934645017 . . . . $8.95

Great Gunfighters of the Old West - 9781681790596 . . . . $12.95

Historic Ranches of the Old West - 9780978915094 . . . . $24.95

John Chisum: Fronier Cattle King - 9781681791135 . . . . $19.95

The Johnson County War - 9781571688767 . . . . $27.95

Lampasas 1855-1895: Biography of a Frontier City - 9781940130637 . . . . . . $24.95

Long Before the Pilgrims
First Thanksgiving, El Paso del Norte 1598 - 9781571684981 . . . . $12.95

Pacific Coast League 1903-1988 - 978-0890157763 . . . . $26.95

Reel Cowboys: Western Movie Stars Who Thrilled Young Fans
and Helped Them Grow Up Decent and Strong - 978-1571683304 . . . . $16.95

Reel Rangers: Texas Rangers in Movies, TV,
Radio & Other Forms of Popular Culture - 9781571688408 . . . . $19.95

Sam Houston: A Study in Leadership - 9781681790374 . . . . $19.95

Sam Houston Slept Here
Homes of the Chief Executives of Texas - 9781571685841 . . . . $19.95

The Sons of the Pioneers - 9781571686442 . . . . $24.95

The Southern League: Baseball in Dixie, 1885-1994 - 978-0890159521 . . . . . $24.95

The Texas League 1888-1987
A Century of Baseball - 978-0890156094 . . . . $24.95

For More Information
www.EakinPress.com • www.WildHorseStore.com

www.ingramcontent.com/pod-product-compliance
Lightning Source LLC
Chambersburg PA
CBHW060051100426
42742CB00014B/2776